Academic Freedom Imperiled

Wilbur S. Shepperson Series in Nevada History

Academic Freedom Imperiled

The McCarthy Era at the University of Nevada

J. Dee Kille

University of Nevada Press ▲▲ Reno & Las Vegas

Wilbur S. Shepperson Series in Nevada History
Series Editor: Michael Green

University of Nevada Press, Reno, Nevada 89557 USA

Manufactured in the United States of America
Design by Carrie House
Library of Congress Cataloging-in-Publication Data
Kille, J. Dee (Jimee Dee), 1949–
Academic freedom imperiled : the McCarthy era at the University of Nevada / J. Dee Kille.
p. cm. — (Wilbur S. Shepperson series in Nevada history)
Includes bibliographical references and index.
ISBN 0-87417-593-3 (hardcover : alk. paper)
1. University of Nevada—History—20th century.
2. Academic freedom—Nevada—Reno—History—20th century. 3. Stout, Minard W. I. Title. II. Series.
LD3763.K55 2004
378.793'55—dc22 2004001808
The paper used in this book meets the requirements of American National Standard for Information Sciences—Permanence of Paper for Printed Library Materials, ANSI Z.48-1984. Binding materials were selected for strength and durability.

FIRST PRINTING
13 12 11 10 09 08 07 06 05 04
5 4 3 2 1

To Fred: Thank you

CONTENTS

ILLUSTRATIONS

ACKNOWLEDGMENTS

This study has benefited from the help and support of many individuals. I wish to express my appreciation for the research assistance given me by Chris Driggs, Jeffrey Kintop, and the staff at the Nevada State Archives, Karen Gash at the University of Nevada Archives, the staff at the University of Nevada Oral History Project, Nan Bowers at the Nevada State Legislative Council Bureau, the staff of the University of Nevada Government Documents Department, and Mike Esposito, who assisted me in my library research. In addition, I wish to extend my appreciation to Dr. Jordan E. Kurland, associate general secretary of the American Association of University Professors (AAUP), whose efforts secured the early release of the AAUP's "University of Nevada" files.

For their time and efforts in reading and editing, I wish to thank Jerome E. Edwards, C. Elizabeth Raymond, James W. Hulse, Robert M. Gorrell, and copy editor Annette Wenda. A special thank-you is due Richard O. Davies, without whose encouragement, support, direction, and persistence this manuscript would not have been completed. Finally, I wish to extend a note of appreciation to Mrs. Margaret Shepperson for her continuous support over the past nine years.

Ultimate thanks, however, goes to Fred Kille for the many hours of patient understanding that he expended in research, reading, editing, rereading, and solace.

Academic Freedom Imperiled

Introduction

Throughout its first six decades in Reno as the only institution of higher learning in the state, the University of Nevada (UN) had experienced a relatively placid existence. From the admission of the first students in 1886 until World War II, the university had evolved into a traditional land-grant institution with particular emphasis upon the liberal arts and sciences along with special professional programs in engineering, mining, agriculture, nursing, and education. It was viewed by the citizenry of the state as a quiet, conservative, and secure place where the relatively small number of college-bound graduates from the state's few high schools could pursue an undergraduate degree, perhaps prepare themselves for admission to law or medical school, but more than likely leave campus prepared to assume a leadership role in their communities. It was not until 1927 that the enrollment reached the magic figure of 1,000, and in 1940, with the state's population hovering at just 110,000, the university enrolled just 1,255 students.[1]

Thus, the small university "up there" on the hill overlooking the small city of Reno fulfilled its modest role—offering basic undergraduate programs, fielding usually underachieving athletic teams, and offering its students a secure and comfortable academic and social environment in the age of in loco parentis. The faculty hired to this frontier academic outpost reflected the social and political conservatism of the community; they taught a standard traditional curriculum and engaged in research that often related to the particular needs of the state. Although the University of Nevada held land-grant status, the tree-lined quadrangle of redbrick buildings gave visitors the distinct impression of an eastern liberal arts college. And indeed the faculty took seriously their responsibilities for providing a sound liberal arts education, carefully sculpting those requirements around the professional curricula that gave testimony to the land-grant obligations. Safe, solid, conservative, and traditional, the university found itself unprepared, both financially and philosophically, to cope with the sudden period of enrollment growth that burst upon the campus in the autumn of 1945 when a flood of veterans came back from the war, armed with the GI Bill and eager to get on with their post-military lives. By the 1947–1948 academic year, enrollment had jumped 36 percent above the prewar figure to 1,974. Not only were the numbers overwhelming, but so too were the expectations and demands of a new type of student—older, focused, career oriented, many recently married, their attitudes and outlooks tempered by the fires of war. These self-assured, mature students had fought for democracy abroad and would accept no less at home; they helped challenge the old conservative order and pushed the university toward becoming a modern, competitive educational institution.

What transpired at UN in the postwar years reflected what was occurring across the land as once quiet campuses became convulsed by enormous enrollment growth.[2] Many institutions were placed under extreme pressures to expand their faculties, modify their curricula, and find monies to build expensive new facilities to meet the needs of enlarged student bodies. The result often was conflict and division as administrators and faculties scrambled to respond to the demands of a new academic era. The ensuing tensions produced by unprecedented growth, however, were greatly exacerbated by national political issues growing out of the cold war. With the United States engaged in a war of competing ideologies, universities naturally became central to national security, not only for their science and engineering capabilities, but also as centers for the study of ideas and values. Historian Ellen Schrecker concludes, "[B]y the 1950s the academy had displaced all other institutions as the locus of America's intellectual life." However, the shrill demands from patriotic and conservative political forces on behalf of ideological purity produced a fundamental conflict between loyalty and freedom of academic expression. As historian William Manchester explains, America's campuses were "torn by a double allegiance, to the flag and to academic freedom."[3]

On the national political front, one of the most important issues of the 1950s was the effort of opportunistic politicians to exploit widespread public fears about the threats posed to U.S. security by the Soviet Union and the international Communist movement. Several shrewd politicians of both parties created the impression that a vast conspiracy existed internally within the United States. The immediate catalyst for this movement, the cold war, pitted the United States and its allies against the Communist forces controlled by the Soviet Union. However, the movement itself had deep and pervasive roots within American life. These included the anti–labor union movement of the late nineteenth century and the Red scare of 1919–1920. This short but important anti-Communist crusade emerged from American fears that developed in the wake of the Russian Revolution, and was cynically led by Democratic presidential hopeful Attorney General A. Mitchell Palmer and his special assistant, J. Edgar Hoover. By the time Senator Joseph McCarthy, a Republican from Wisconsin, sought to exploit fears of Communist influence within the United States for his own political benefit in 1950, the excesses and devastation wrought by the Red scare had largely faded from public memory. Between 1950 and 1954, however, McCarthy became a powerful and much feared political force as he manipulated public opinion and the national media to mislead millions of citizens into believing that the nation was imperiled by Communists deeply entrenched in U.S. government agencies (especially the State Department), labor unions, and university and college faculty. As many scholars have demonstrated, one of the devastating impacts of his irrational political movement was to reduce the level of discourse about U.S. foreign policy and security matters in Congress as well as among the general public. Many believe that McCarthyism had a distinctly chilling effect upon the willingness of America's intellectuals to examine and discuss the perceived Communist infiltration of American life and the threats it posed to national security (and there was evidence that these threats did exist). Many also believe that this freedom of open discussion and discourse—academic freedom—was seriously eroded as a result of McCarthy's ruthless crusade.

The issues of McCarthyism, academic freedom, and the right of students and faculty to participate in their own governance became the vortex around which the controversies of the 1950s spun on the campus of one small western state university. In examining the academic freedom controversy at the University of Nevada in the 1950s, it was obvious that many of the same attitudes about American values and identity prevailed that were dominant during the Red scare of the late teens and early 1920s, the Great Depression of the 1930s, and the terrorism at the turn of the twenty-first century. Paralleling those attitudes, the definition of and the support for academic freedom followed a similar cyclical pattern. Thus, changes in the definition of academic freedom were often made in response to external pressures rather than to campus concerns. In response to these increasing external pressures during times of national crisis, university administrations often redefined the boundaries of academic freedom to bring it into closer compliance.

At the end of the nineteenth century, academic freedom had yet to be codified into formal, but malleable, parameters. But one consistent fact informed academic freedom from its inception: campus problems were best resolved by the academy itself. Hence, as the modern university structure began developing in the late nineteenth century, administrators reinforced their prerogative to resolve internal campus problems. As outside pressures increased in response to social, cultural, or political uncertainty, however, administrators redefined academic freedom as a way to maintain their autonomy. Perhaps it was this earlier mode of administration by which Minard W. Stout attempted to govern the University of Nevada in the 1950s. He strongly advocated the generally accepted principle that on-campus decisions were best made by those who ran the campus. It was conventional wisdom for him, as it had been for Nicholas Murray Butler of Columbia University and other early twentieth-century presidents, that as president he had the technical expertise to understand and solve academic problems.

The founding of the American Association of University Professors (AAUP) by John Dewey, E. R. A. Seligman, Richard T. Ely, and Arthur O. Lovejoy in 1915 was, according to historian Ellen Schrecker, predicated more on "developing professional standards" than on "protecting colleagues from politically inspired dismissals." The AAUP's 1915 report contained in those standards a "set of norms for college teachers which, if followed, would entitle them to the protection of academic freedom." The report further made clear that one of the purposes for defining academic freedom was for the protection of the "overall status, security, and prestige of the academic profession" from outside meddling.[4] Thus, the AAUP, in the same vein as the campus administrators, believed that academic discipline problems should be resolved by the academic profession. Unlike administrators, however, the association believed that investigations and disciplinary actions required the input of the faculty, not just the administration. As a result, the AAUP, too, in its effort to keep outside policing at bay, had to modify its definition of academic freedom as new issues arose that threatened the academic profession.

The local nature of and the focus on faculty discipline in the controversy at UN in the 1950s should have been what Schrecker refers to as merely the "ordinary background noise of academic life; the kinds of conflicts that were endemic to the heterogeneous nature of American higher education."[5] However, the widespread attention focused on university and college campuses generated by the Red scare as well as the McCarthy and House Un-American Activities Committee (HUAC) investigations propelled UN into the national spotlight, along with many other campuses that shared similar problems. The incident would have been no less significant for the participants had national exposure not existed. But the exposure bolstered both sides and in the end probably brought about a quicker resolution.

It was within this larger national context that the University of Nevada found itself embroiled in an intense controversy that threatened its academic integrity and even raised concerns about its future as a viable academic institution. When pragmatic midwesterner Minard W. Stout was appointed as president by the Board of Regents in 1952, the stage was set. The leadership of the board made it clear to their new president that he was to bring a small cadre of outspoken faculty members into line. Those individuals in question were mostly relatively new to Nevada, having received advanced degrees from some of the nation's most prominent institutions where, among other things, they became imbued with the importance of shared governance. In an institutional setting that lacked a meaningful faculty organization, and with key committees controlled by administrators, the faculty naturally chafed under their own lack of influence in developing institutional policies and in making important curricular and personnel decisions. By demanding an expanded role in policy making, the faculty threatened the traditional top-down control of the campus long held by the conservative Board of Regents. When the new president—whose outlook mirrored that of the board—shortly after his arrival on campus took drastic action to punish a small number of dissident faculty in the Departments of English and Biology, the university was thrown into an academic and legal maelstrom that forever changed the nature of the institution. The ensuing controversy lasted for five years, propelling the campus and the larger Nevada community into a no-holds-barred struggle. Resolution of the conflict was ultimately determined by decisions made far beyond the campus, in the courts and in the Nevada state legislature.

The external force that created more havoc with the internal functioning of colleges and universities than any other was fear of Communist infiltration. McCarthyism, then cresting at its zenith nationwide, provided the prism through which this campus controversy was viewed and interpreted. Although the faculty members identified for termination were never formally charged with Communist connections, they were early on painted by their accusers with the Red brush of Communism. Their heretical views, however, proved to be only "dangerous thoughts" that threatened the power of the Board of Regents by seeking to open up the small university to meaningful faculty dialogue and involvement in making important decisions.

Thus, the University of Nevada was plunged into a period of great turmoil that would ultimately be prominently discussed on the front pages of national newspapers and in magazines. It led to censure by the American Association of University Professors, and it prompted several of UN's most prominent faculty to go elsewhere to pursue academic careers. The dissension bitterly polarized the campus as well as its alumni and community supporters. It ultimately produced a statewide political controversy that was resolved only by the departure of the contentious president, the retirement of the board's powerful chairman, and the restructuring of the board itself by the state legislature.

In today's crisis atmosphere created by terrorism's challenge to American society, culture, and values, outside pressures are once again making their presence felt. As during earlier crises, campus administrators are attempting to protect the academy from those pressures. For example, the president of a California community college issued a memo "warning professors not to discuss the current war in their classrooms," and an "alumni association of a prestigious, private New England university rescinded an award to a graduating senior who joined a protest against President [George W.] Bush's visit to campus." The AAUP, too, is attempting to keep the issues of academic discipline within the authority of the academic profession. The association, though aware that there have been very few overt threats to academic freedom, has warned of the "need to maintain a close watch on the situation" and has stepped up its monitoring because of an increase in "a variety of subtler dangers." The association's concern is supported by a *Chronicle of Higher Education* report that "professors who criticize the U.S. government or society find little tolerance of their views" and that "faculty members across the country have found their freedom to speak out hemmed in by incensed students, alumni, and university officials."[6]

Academic freedom recurrently faces challenges similar to those that occurred during earlier eras of national crisis. By studying the ramifications of earlier confrontations, one can gain insight into how better to interpret and resolve contemporary conflicts. Thus, a study of the academic freedom imbroglio at the University of Nevada during the 1950s not only helps define these issues, but also reaffirms that controversy can, indeed, be progressive.

1: Dictators and "Reducators"

"I guess you're all wondering what kind of S.O.B. I am." This was exactly the statement with which Minard W. Stout opened his first faculty meeting on September 12, 1952. For the faculty members, whether they had been wondering or not, the remainder of Stout's address clarified matters. He stated that "he assumed that all faculty members felt that a president had to be some kind of overbearing character to get to be president. . . . While that might be true, he would try to make himself clear and understood at all times. . . . To be a president, you might have to be rough at times." Upon completion of his speech, he immediately left the room without acknowledging the faculty, neither asking for their reactions nor answering questions. On that late-summer day, the new president of the University of Nevada left no doubt that he was a man on a mission. Stout, in a 1972 interview, confirmed that he had, indeed, been given a mandate by the Board of Regents to "clean things up."[1]

Minard Stout was the new presidential choice of the Board of Regents, which had decided, according to Chairman Silas Ross, that the position should seek the man. In executive session, the regents dictated the specifications required for the man hired to replace Malcolm Love as president of the university. The stated position description was quite conventional: the successful candidate must have a degree from an institution of the same rating as UN, at least three years' teaching experience during the past five, and administrative experience. The successful candidate must also be familiar with the West and have an appreciation of the role of the university and of the land-grant concept. Finally, he must be a family man between the ages of forty and fifty-five.[2] What remained unstated, however, was more significant than what was made public. The regents, by seeking recommendations from other university presidents, could specify additional qualifications, such as a commitment to a strong presidency and the centralization of decision making. That the regents believed they had hired the "hardnose" they needed was made obvious in their agreement to let Stout be his "own man," to let him bring in his own lieutenants, and not to tell him what to do. As events soon revealed, Stout's philosophy coincided with that espoused by Chairman Ross in 1945—that faculty should "stick to their classes" and do the work for which they were hired, that is, teach and not involve themselves in the governance of the university.[3]

At the beginning of the 1950s, the Board of Regents and the president of the University of Nevada, in response to the rapid, chaotic, and foreboding postwar changes, wanted to maintain a firm hold on the university's traditional past while the rest of the state was struggling to move forward into a dynamic new era. But, regardless of tradition, the university, like many other agencies in the state, was reluctantly dragged into what Governor Charles H. Russell referred to as "this new period of meeting the now existing national and world responsibility."[4]

Between 1940 and 1950, Nevada's population increased from 110,000 to 160,000, and the growth rate accelerated as the decade wore on. By 1955, the population stood at 245,000; as the 1950s closed, however, with a population of 285,000 (most of whom lived in Reno and Las Vegas), Nevada had become the fastest-growing state in the nation.[5] Many who came to Nevada during the 1950s were seeking employment in the growing casino and tourist industries. Legalized gambling, officially denigrated by the rest of the country as disreputable and even sinful, was not viewed that way by average Nevada residents. The decadent and sometimes "dangerous" reputation of the casinos in Las Vegas's loud and gaudy Glitter Gulch and along its flashy Strip was a siren song to those who wanted to add excitement to their lives and, they hoped, money to their pockets. But Nevada was not merely a mecca for the gambler who thought he could beat the system and the eastern mobster who was milking that system. The state was developing into a viable region where small entrepreneurs, professionals, and average working people came for opportunities to build a life amid the increasing development and the growing service economy. In the northern part of the state, Reno's and Lake Tahoe's less flashy casinos provided a more homey and traditional atmosphere in which people could feel a sense of belonging.

Indeed, Reno, thanks to the presence of the University of Nevada, exuded a "college town" atmosphere. That more people preferred Reno and Lake Tahoe as places to spend the six-week waiting period for divorces than Las Vegas was indicative of the difference in lifestyle and pace between the two metropolitan centers of the state. A second burgeoning source of employment was the state's emphasis on ever increasing tourism, including its active development and promotion of an outdoor recreation industry.[6] The dichotomy between northern and southern Nevada was represented in this new industry. Las Vegas, in addition to indoor sports and golf, could offer only Lake Mead and the Hoover Dam as tourist attractions. Reno and Lake Tahoe had a wide variety of both winter and summer outdoor activities and a background landscape of the mythic West to vary the visitors' experiences and prolong their stay. Reno and Las Vegas were both able to take advantage of a fairly stable population of military personnel from Stead Air Force Base and Nellis Air Force Base. The increased presence of military facilities provided an economic base in Nevada and brought a new group of semi-permanent residents, many of whom would remain in the Silver State after their tours of duty.

By the time Stout arrived, the rapidly increasing number of new Nevadans in these two metropolitan areas had taken an active interest in the economic, political, and social decision-making processes at all levels in their community. Many were making their presence felt at the state level as well. Many of the young graduates of UN were building their future political careers as well as actively participating in the affairs of their alma mater. The rural conservative presence, however, was not to be denied. In an effort to keep political power in the hands of the traditional power structure, that is, the rural and small-town elite, a constitutional amendment was passed in 1950 that based the state senate on one representative from each county.[7] Thus, the more diverse and progressive metropolitan centers with large populations were limited in their ability to influence the actions of the legislature.

Despite the huge influx of new voters and the growing demands for a strong faculty role on the university campus, those who wanted to make changes in the political structure and ideology of Nevada faced a long uphill battle. According to the historian Russell Elliott, by the early 1960s, the rural counties still controlled the operation of the state, even though they contained a minority of the population. Because each county was allowed only one state senator, a mere "eight percent of the voters . . . [were] capable of electing a majority [nine] of the seventeen-member state senate." In addition, the state's apportionment system was structured such that "21.1 percent of the voters could elect over 50 percent of the thirty-seven-member assembly."[8] But these daunting barriers did not impede new independent-minded Nevadans from working toward changing their state's governing philosophy.

By 1959, Washoe and Clark Counties together accounted for 75 percent of all inhabitants; Las Vegas replaced Reno as the state's largest city. The new citizens were mostly young people looking to incorporate their own postwar ideologies into the social and political structure of the state. By about the middle of the decade, 75 percent of Nevada's residents were less than forty-five years of age. The educational level of Nevadans in general was third highest in the western region.[9] As a result, the rapidly changing personality of the state could not help but be reflected in the microcosm of the state's only university.

After the war, by the late 1940s, the nature of faculty and students at the university had entered a period of rapid and disconcerting change. The war against totalitarianism in Europe had reinforced the ideas of democracy here at home. Many of the younger faculty, who had come to Nevada from prestigious liberal arts institutions located in more cosmopolitan areas, brought with them their own ideas of democracy and shared faculty governance. The influx of former GIs into the student ranks created a demand for personal accountability and student participation in the running of their campus. Both of these factors were diametrically opposed to the administration's efforts to maintain its firm control over all things important on campus. That Nevada's two traditional primary businesses, agriculture and mining, were being displaced by expanding tourist-based economies and a more diverse citizenry created a new set of expectations. These statewide changes were reflected on campus. It was thus in the context of a rapidly changing state demographic composition that Minard Stout sought to adhere to an administrative style that an increasing number of faculty believed was no longer appropriate.

Immediately prior to taking the helm at UN, Stout had served as the director of a laboratory school at the University of Minnesota. His qualifications and experiences were bounded by his midwestern heritage and education. He had earned his B.A. in economics from the University of Northern Iowa in 1929, his M.A. in political science from the University of Iowa in 1933, and his Ph.D. in administration at the University of Iowa in 1943. His experience included stints as teacher and principal of a high school in Iowa, and principal of both the University of Iowa and the University of Minnesota laboratory high schools where he also trained student teachers and taught courses in educational administration. His military experience from 1943 to 1945 was at the command level. Stout's education prepared him to be an administrator; the effect of his experience equipped him to be insensitive to the needs of subordinates. He defined his administrative philosophy in the hierarchical dictum that corresponded to Plato's *Myth of the Metals.* Stout explained Plato's managerial classification system in the following terms: "Some have the power to command; and these [God] has made of gold; others of silver, to be auxiliaries; others again, who are to be husbandmen and craftsmen, he has made of brass and iron." That all of the positions Stout held were golden ones militated against a successful experience in leading university faculties, especially those from the liberal arts area. He apparently did not recognize that there was a significant difference between administering in the highly structured public school milieu and the more self-governing atmosphere of higher education. Paralleling that outlook was a lack of commitment to what local physician and UN supporter Fred Anderson called the "Academic Holy Trinity" of "tenure, academic freedom of speech and research, and faculty participation in university decisions and governance."[10]

Stout relied upon his previous experiences to determine how a university should operate. His method of choice, undoubtedly with encouragement and support from the regents, was a strident version of a top-down chain of command. Stout's conservative, business-inspired governing philosophy was initially well received throughout most of the state. As James W. Hulse writes, "Stout was remarkably successful in dealing with the conservative regents who selected him and the initial responses of the community, the press, and the legislature were favorable." In fact, shortly after his arrival, he toured the state in order to gain support for his goals. He acquired a better understanding of rural Nevada. The attention he gave to the small-town boosters and service clubs, as well as to the ranching organizations, helped strengthen statewide ties to the university and, not incidentally, to Stout personally. During these meetings, he put forth his administrative philosophy that was very much in accord with local convictions. He solidified the nexus with the local powers by inviting their input and promising not only to be an advocate for their children, but also to improve instruction at UN by bringing in top-notch instructors and expanding research into local needs; for a clincher, he promised to rebuild the sagging athletic program.[11] The president's emphasis on getting top instructors to come to the university could be interpreted as a veiled warning that existing faculty who were not "doing their job" would be replaced.

Although a strong presidency was not a foreign concept to the faculty and staff at UN, Stout's narrow interpretation and draconian application of it immediately alienated many of them. He estranged them further by sharply curtailing, and in some cases eliminating, traditional avenues of faculty participation in governance such as the faculty committee. He took these steps because "he favored 'an administration as simple as possible' and he considered the university to be a 'community of scholars and felt the academic council system was set up to bypass the administrators.'" For Stout, according to one professor, the very idea of committees as viable, functioning bodies was ludicrous because, in his opinion, "you cannot pool ignorance and come up with knowledge." Consequently, Stout's "simplification" of the university administration took the form of a basic corporate-style hierarchical flow chart with discretionary power devolving downward and nothing evolving upward; his most significant changes came under the heading of "committees." In the revised procedures submitted by Stout to the Board of Regents, the phase "An Administrator may appoint committees to advise him or to aid him in carrying out his duties" made plain that faculty committees would be called only at the pleasure of the administration and that their "advice" need not be taken.[12] Because of his own experience, Stout was unable to recognize that, in the university environment of the 1950s, such an abridgement of faculty involvement would not go unchallenged.

If the president, from his experience in institutions of higher learning, understood the concept of academic freedom as it is defined in the university community, he chose to apply it selectively. Academic freedom as defined by the American Association of University Professors means that a teacher is entitled to freedom in the classroom in discussing his or her subject, but he or she should be careful not to introduce into the teaching controversial matter that has no relation to the subject. In addition, the AAUP has decreed that the faculty has primary responsibility for such fundamental areas as curriculum, subject matter, methods of instruction and research, faculty status, and those aspects of student life that relate to the educational process.[13] Stout was a firm advocate of academic freedom in the classroom. In fact, he insisted that faculty stick to their areas and teach only those subjects for which they were trained. However, the second part of the definition, that faculty should participate in institutional decision making, was completely foreign and extraneous to his ideology.

Consequently, Stout's personal philosophy and his "mandate" from the Board of Regents led him to immediately assail academic freedom in two ways. First, his laudable but unrealistic conviction that the "principles of democratic education required that all graduates of high schools be given an opportunity to do university work" led him to demand the relaxation of entrance requirements.[14] Second, he stifled faculty input by circumventing and later eliminating the Academic Council and other faculty governance bodies. By these moves, Stout assured himself of a sharp reaction not only from the faculty, but eventually from the state legislature and the community at large as well.

One of the first issues tackled by President Stout upon his arrival in 1952 was that of halting a declining enrollment caused, in part, by the decreasing number of World War II veterans taking advantage of the GI Bill. As more and more GIs finished their educations and began their careers in the outside world, enrollment figures for Nevada dropped sharply from 1,974 in 1948 to 1,239 when Stout took the reins in the fall of 1952. The GI Bill would not kick in again until the Korean War veterans began returning to campus in 1954. In the meantime, in order to maintain funding and keep the university at a high level of production, Stout had much work to do to find ways to increase enrollment. He believed that he could solve the problem by relying on his long-held belief in democratically extending a university education to all high school graduates. Stout espoused a "triangular philosophy of education" that included a belief in the worth of the student, an understanding that he is different from each of the others, and the need to create a learning environment that would encourage his optimum growth as an individual and as a member of society. In promoting this philosophy, Stout reopened the heated debate over entrance requirements. His proposed policy of allowing all Nevada high school graduates to enroll regardless of their grades or course work had been tried at UN between 1946 and 1950. By 1949, according to James Hulse, "the lower standards had produced so many problems that there was a general movement in the University, supported by secondary school principals and teachers, to reimpose the more rigid admission requirements. The faculty [agreed and] voted to do so in 1950."[15] However, drawing on his own studies of other universities, Stout insisted that UN's entrance requirements were more stringent than those of comparable institutions. He told faculty that he was going to recommended to the regents that UN institute a system of relaxed entrance requirements and once again admit "unclassified" students. It was this issue that led to the major confrontation on the Nevada campus in 1953.

Before submitting his proposal, however, Stout requested the Admissions Committee to review the current admission requirements and advise him on how his proposal would impact the university. The amount of authority Stout had over his committees was made evident in a letter from Admissions Committee chairman William Smyth to Dean Fredrick Wood, chairman of the Academic Council, in January 1953. Smyth related that the only point the committee members objected to (and did so unanimously) was the deletion of the clause "Unclassified students shall not represent the University of Nevada in inter-collegiate events." But, he continued, after Stout assured him that the unclassified-student category would not be used as a means to recruit athletes, the committee agreed to the removal of the clause.[16] Given Stout's public promise to rebuild the intercollegiate athletic teams at UN, the committee must have had unshakable faith in the president's word.

On January 17, 1953, the Admissions Committee submitted the results of its study on lowering entrance requirements and, on April 10, "without consulting the entire faculty, Stout obtained the Regents' approval for new and lower admission standards." Although the committee's report was presented to the regents as unanimous, there was a disclaimer appended to the end. The committee believed that because many students who would be admitted under these lower standards made "a satisfactory record only rarely," their disaffection did "no good either for them or the University." Further, it recommended that a special study be undertaken to determine the type of program, personnel, or facilities these individuals would need, and "whether or not the program should be put into effect."[17]

Stout further justified his admission plan in an address before the local chapter of the AAUP at which time he invited input from anyone who had access to research data contrary to his own. This action seemed to open the president's proposal to debate, and Frank Richardson, chair of the Department of Biology and president of the local chapter of the AAUP, took up the offer. He distributed copies of "Aimlessness in Education," an article by University of Illinois history professor Arthur E. Bestor Jr., which, in addition to being critical of lowering admission requirements, was also critical of "educationists."[18] This latter point, though not the focus of Richardson's intent, was certainly not overlooked. Richardson sent approximately thirty copies of the article to faculty members, chairs, deans, and, in an effort to be fair and open in the debate, Stout with a "special note of explanation" appended.[19] Because open debate was not what Stout had intended, he immediately moved to bring the recalcitrant into line.

It was not just because the Bestor article criticized Stout's admission policies, but also that Stout interpreted it to be an intentional disparagement of the administration and of the professors of the School of Education that caused him to chastise Richardson. The article itself discusses the difference between the classical form of education and the post-Dewey pragmatic focus on "real-life problems." For Bestor, a classic or "genuine education" is one built around "the liberal disciplines" that are the "powerful tools and engines by which a man discovers and handles facts" and have been the pillar of American education. Bestor decries the encroachment of "merely a gaudy show," teaching based on solving "real-life problems" as represented in "athletic games, camping, collecting art objects, etc., and doing parlor stunts." The major portion of Bestor's article examines this aspect of the argument between knowledge and "know-how." Very little actual mention is made of relaxing college entrance requirements and the effects such a move would have on education. Bestor, however, implies that while lowering college entrance requirements in order to accept students with substandard grades is bad enough, lowering them to admit students who have taken only "real-life" courses will be devastating to America's educational standing. He believes that the drift toward "aimlessness" in education is caused by public education moving away from teaching liberal arts knowledge and into providing "real-life" know-how. Bestor condemns professors of education, school administrators, and state and federal officials as the source of the aimlessness behind the lowering of entrance requirements.[20] Such was not the case in Nevada; the rejection of lower standards by Nevada public school officials in 1950 and the high level of integrity of the administration and faculty of UN's School of Education challenged Bestor's contention.

Nonetheless, in response to both Richardson's interference and the presumed insult, on November 19, 1952, President Stout called him into his office to discuss the competence of the article's author, to find out why the biologist had distributed the article, and to point out that Richardson had broken the chain of command. Because Stout had his secretary, Alice Terry, take minutes of that meeting, there is a stenographic record that preserves the discussion. In addition, because he had his secretary take notes, he intentionally created a threatening environment for Richardson. This method of adding pressure and intimidation to the subject of a disciplinary discussion was an effective favorite of his. Stout would later use it on Rollan Melton, a student and reporter for the campus newspaper, the *U of N Sagebrush,* who wrote an article favorable to Richardson. On another occasion, he added a variation to this menacing weapon. James Hulse, a reporter for the *Nevada State Journal* during Stout's administration, relates that during an interview in which he was accused of "snooping," the president surreptitiously reached into his desk drawer and clicked something.[21] Whether the president was actually tape-recording the conversation or not, the intent was clearly intimidation, and the effect was to stifle free speech.

Among the important points of Bestor's article about which Stout and Richardson disagreed was the author's qualifications to write an article critical of admission standards. Richardson believed Bestor was competent because he had long experience in higher education and because admission qualifications were a topic of vital interest to all academics. Stout, on the other hand, insisted that because Bestor was not trained in education and educational administration, he was in no way qualified to write the article. Because "the article was critical of professors of education and public school administrators, charging that they evaded their responsibilities by eliminating 'scholastic discipline' subjects," Stout argued that ridicule of the School of Education and its professors was the reason Richardson distributed the article. Near the end of the meeting, Stout lectured Richardson on how the university was to be run and the proper place of faculty.

> Dr. Richardson, this is serious, because on this campus there is not going to be any departmental friction. There is going to be no case of any department belittling or criticizing others. . . . In case there is any individual who feels he has to stir up friction, then he is going to leave the faculty. . . . You were hired to teach biology. This year you were

> given the appointment to serve as department head. That does not make you a critic or supervisor of the entire program of higher education. . . . I believe in having experts who know their fields and who have the judgement to stick to their fields.[22]

On the topic of admission requirements, the reason for the distribution of the article in the first place, Richardson reemphasized that admission standards were an area of concern for all members of the university, both faculty and administration. Stout's view of who controlled admission standards, however, is obvious in his reply: "Frankly, that is none of your business. That rests in the hands of the regents." When Richardson insisted that admission standards did affect him, especially as they impacted the "quality of students and their attitudes," Stout issued the line that made him famous in several magazines across the land: "You are hired to teach biology and not to be a buttinsky all over the campus." He elaborated on his point that the regents and he were the bosses and that Richardson was the hired employee. "I think certain things have to be pointed out to you. . . . If you are not happy in the job that is assigned to you we will help you move, but as long as you stay here we will ask you for help in other areas when we need it. That is all."[23]

Over the course of the next several months, the relationship between Stout and Richardson worsened, which, in turn, affected the entire faculty. On February 18, the president summoned a general faculty meeting at which, in a "cold rage," he denounced faculty members for intruding into his administrative domain. He ended the tirade with the bold threat that "I was taught to fight fair and to fight foul and I can fight foul." Several faculty members and even the Faculty Welfare Committee, or, to use Stout's turn of phrase, the "wailing wall," attempted to settle the issue between Richardson and the president. Professor Robert Gorrell of the English department and Maurice Beesley, professor of mathematics and chairman of the Faculty Welfare Committee, believed they had the matter settled because Stout agreed not to fire Richardson and Richardson agreed to settle without getting an apology for being threatened with termination of his position.[24] However, the situation continued to deteriorate and, as the later developments indicate, not only was the Richardson-Stout issue not settled, it had also expanded.

Richardson's challenge to authority and Stout's retaliation attracted the attention of state legislators who were hearing "persistent reports that 'something is wrong at the University of Nevada.'" Whatever the source of the reports reaching the state assembly, their content was such that Speaker M. E. McCuistion, on March 10, 1953, appointed Assemblymen G. William Coulthard of Las Vegas, James E. Wood of Washoe County, and F. E. Walters of

Elko County to an investigating committee to identify the nature of the problems and get the university back on track. The committee was given one week to "probe reports of dissension between students and faculty, faculty and department heads and between the faculty and the president and the regents."[25]

That the assembly would interfere in the domain of the regents struck many as a political maneuver intended to increase legislative control over the administration of the university. An editorial in the March 12, 1953, issue of the *Reno Evening Gazette* pointed out the ludicrous nature of the investigation. The vagueness of the charge that "all is not well at the university," the anonymous nature of those making the complaints, the short remainder of the legislative session, and the "hit-and-run" character of the investigation all militated against a successful study. The editorial further implied that the entire scenario was politically motivated and would do more harm than good. Although the editor of the *Elko Independent* observed a political angle emanating from the legislative study and resented the intrusion because the legislature had no business investigating the "official university family's affairs," he also believed that the "brief peek" would be sufficient to ferret out the "few disgruntled staff members [who] were the cause of most of the trouble."[26]

After meeting with many faculty and administrators, the Coulthard Committee made the determination that the policy changes instituted by President Stout had "met with general faculty approval" with the result that "relations between the president, deans and department heads and faculty seemed generally good." In the committee's judgment, the problems stemmed from a "small dissident group" of faculty, and it recommended that the president and regents handle this personnel matter expeditiously so that no serious harm or discredit would befall the university. Stout immediately took the Coulthard Committee report to be an affirmation of his methodology and issued letters to the five faculty members he deemed the troublemakers, demanding that they present themselves before the Board of Regents to "show cause" why they should retain their positions. The fact that Coulthard issued a public letter to the two Reno newspapers on April 27, 1953, clearly stating that the report was "intended only to state facts" and "not as an attempt to result in the dismissal of any member of the faculty" seemed to escape the notice of both Stout and the regents.[27]

During the last week of March, when the campus was closed for spring break, the five tenured faculty—Frank Richardson and Thomas Little of the biology department and Robert Gorrell, Charlton Laird, and Robert Hume of the English department—each received identical letters that charged them with "engaging in 'disturbing activities' over a period of 'several years.'" Stout enumerated six alleged activities, including attempts to develop friction between departments and between the university and public schools, falsifying information about the abolition of faculty committees, falsifying information about the lowering of academic standards, falsely accusing the administration of mistreating the faculty, and, perhaps most important for Stout, circumventing the chain of command by alarming the faculty, townspeople, and legislators without first going to and through the administration.[28]

Stout's self-assured, abrasive manner, more than his accusations, engendered much faculty animosity and intensified their response to his actions. The five accused faculty were surprised to have been singled out and confused by the vagueness of the allegations. In point of fact, however, in 1945, shortly after he arrived at Nevada from Cornell University, Gorrell and a few other recently hired professors began pushing for an increased role for faculty in the governance of the university. It was Gorrell and a "nucleus" of "new faculty," including Richardson from the University of California at Berkeley and Laird from Stanford University, who were responsible for creating in the professoriate a "growing . . . awareness of the faculty . . . as a power." In fact, Gorrell attributes the ultimate hiring of Stout to the increasing effectiveness of faculty force in governance.[29] Perhaps Stout was not totally incorrect in his identification of that "small dissident group."

The five were ordered to appear before the Board of Regents on April 10 to show cause why they should not be fired. The professors, however, appealed to the Nevada Supreme Court. The court issued a writ of prohibition ordering the regents to present a bill of particulars by May 7 outlining the charges against the five. However, before the May 7 deadline, charges were dropped against four of the five, leaving only Richardson as the focus of Stout's ire. There was never any satisfactory explanation offered for why the charges against Thomas Little were withdrawn; he "simply received a letter from Stout informing him the charges which accused all of insubordination had been dropped in his case." It is possible that because he had been awarded an Atomic Energy Commission (AEC) research grant in the amount of eighty-two hundred dollars to study radiation effects on plant life, the administration did not want to risk losing the money or the status. There is some validity to this argument, given the fact that the *Reno Evening Gazette* announced the award in its April 18, 1953, issue, and then in the April 27 issue mentioned that the charges against Little had been withdrawn. Mary Ellen Glass, however, believes that "Little used his connections with the American Association of University Professors to convince Stout and his advisors to rescind his dismissal."[30] Regardless of what explanation is chosen for Little's amnesty, the real factor in the entire situation was that Richardson was the only one of the five against whom the administration had any concrete evidence, namely, the dissemination of the Bestor article. But that did not mean the other four came through the ordeal unscathed.

Gorrell believes that in dismissing the charges against the three English professors, Stout either acted disingenuously or perhaps had misunderstood what the regents wanted. In individual conferences with the three, "Stout was just sweet as pie"; he indicated that he wanted only harmony and had been trying to "take care of things between the Board and the University" and "wanted to reinstate us . . . back in good standing." The three professors accepted the offer because they thought the same scenario was being offered to Richardson and Little and that the campus would soon return to normal. But Stout did not offer the two biology professors the same opportunity. Despite the clever way Stout managed to split the cohesiveness of the five, Gorrell believes that Stout was just the errand boy for the board. He recognizes that Stout was brought in to bring the faculty into line, but believes that he was taking his marching orders directly from the regents, Chairman Silas Ross in particular. Gorrell has come to the conclusion that Stout really did not quite know the reason he had sent the show-cause letters, but "that it was Si Ross who had *told* him what to do." He supports his theory with the evidence that after Stout had met with the three English professors and told them all was fine and they would be reinstated, he had to call them back and insist that they make concessions and sign a letter acceding to the authority of the president and the board.[31]

A second factor that confuses the issue of whether Stout or the board was dictating the rules is that all five of the professors were left off the "salary list, which was compiled before the professors were notified of the dismissal hearings." The final salary schedule was approved at the April 10–11 Board of Regents meeting, which, coincidentally, was also the meeting at which the five were supposed to defend themselves. On the published list, the five professors' names were missing, while an associate professor position and an assistant professor position in biology and two professor positions and one associate professor position in English were shown without names and showing no salary increase.[32] Thus, the five positions remained in the budget, but were listed as being unfilled. Whether Stout left the names off when the list was created or whether the regents removed them is unknown. But in either event, such an omission led many to believe that the president and the board had already decided the outcome of the hearings. Gorrell, Laird, and Hume soon realized that Stout's promise of being "reinstated . . . back in good standing" meant that once they had signed the letters of agreement, they had to accept his autocratic control or resign.

The ramifications of where a faculty member stood on the Stout-Richardson issue were made plain at pay-raise time. Gorrell relates with some irony that being reinstated "in good standing" for the three English professors meant that they were not awarded salary increases for the next year. Gorrell felt further alienated when he discovered that those who had testified for the administration later during the Richardson hearing were given "whopping" salary increases. The three, along with Little, were eventually reinstated on the salary list and received the approval of the regents. But Little received no increase at all; Gorrell, Laird, and Hume received about half the amount of the increase given Charles Hicks, a history professor who testified on behalf of the administration.[33]

The salary actions of the board made it obvious that the termination of the five was a foregone conclusion and probably had been from the moment Stout issued the show-cause letters. The observation of another faculty member at the time supports the theory that at least three of the five had been earmarked for termination because they had consistently refused to follow the chain of command. Everett W. Harris, a mechanical engineering professor from 1938 to 1967, believes that Stout was hired by the regents because Chairman Silas Ross "was angered at a small group—primarily English professors"—who spoke up in faculty meetings, "were more politic," and prevented "some things the president [Malcolm Love] wanted." To add weight to this assessment is Gorrell's own admission that during the late 1940s, he and several other "new" English faculty helped reorganize and put teeth into the local chapter of the AAUP.[34] Statements by Stout in 1972 that the board gave him autonomy to run things his own way are in opposition to those of faculty who believed he was doing the board's bidding. Consequently, the differing perspectives make the issue of who was the ultimate autocrat, Stout or Ross, unclear. The results, however, show that whatever criterion was chosen to explain the working relationship between the Board of Regents and President Stout, in the final analysis, the alliance probably rested on a meeting of like minds. The regents were businessmen with very little academic background but much practical experience in chain-of-command business organizations. The president, although more experienced with the academy, was also steeped in the tradition of top-down management. His academic training reinforced that theory because his skills had been put to the service of training administrators to run institutions autocratically, not democratically.

The treatment of Harold Brown, chair of the Department of Education at UN, demonstrated that the administration was capable of reacting with righteous indignation when its authority was thwarted. According to a *Nevada State Journal* article, as one of the recipients of a copy of "Aimlessness in Education" sent by Richardson, Brown was initially disturbed by Bestor's one-sided, negative approach to the field of teaching education and education administration. He immediately contacted Richardson, and their discussion of the article was "hot and heavy." But in the end, Richardson convinced Brown that the goal in sending the article was to point out the dangers in lowering admission requirements, not to belittle either Brown or his department. Brown, a firm believer in academic freedom, testified during the hearing that although he would not have chosen either the article or the method of distribution, he believed that the biologist "had a right to circulate the article."[35] Brown's integrity was destined to get him into trouble with both Stout and the regents' attorneys, but it would take its toll on the administration's public image as well.

Because Brown was a professor of education, Stout assumed that he would be outraged by the article, and therefore a willing witness against Richardson. In early May, Stout sent Arts and Science dean Fredrick Wood to ask Brown to meet with the regents' attorneys. Brown, who bore no malice toward either side, wished to remain neutral. Wood informed Brown that neutrality was not an option and passed along the dictum that "[e]veryone is going to be stood up and counted." To this threat, Brown replied, "If I am going to be asked to testify against my convictions, I'll see a lawyer." The interesting choice of words employed by Wood made it plain that he was bearing a message from the administration. Inherent in that message was that an accounting was being made among faculty to determine who was on which side. At a second meeting later that day, Brown told Wood that if called, he would testify willingly. Wood, realizing that Brown's integrity would lead him to testify for the defense, accused him of being "uncooperative like another department head, Frank Richardson."[36]

Brown did testify for Richardson and by doing so showed the administration that his principles were stronger than their absolutism and that no one was going to impair his academic freedom or his integrity. What the administration saw, however, was that Brown was, indeed, uncooperative, had refused to go through proper channels, and had directly obstructed the boss's directives. Once again, the supreme power of authoritarianism was displayed for those who refused to see the light. Brown not only took a cut in salary by losing his summer school directorship, but was also passed over for the deanship when the School of Education was upgraded to a college.[37]

By the time the public hearing began on May 25, 1953, a local league of socially prominent citizens and political hopefuls had decided to challenge Stout and the regents. Through their efforts, these "Friends of the University" disseminated information throughout the United States and, in return, garnered the public support of universities and colleges nationwide. The Richardson case became a national cause célébre and put UN on the front pages across the land. The Friends of the University's actions were instrumental in bringing the case to the attention of other academics, but a major reason that a relatively obscure case from a provincial Nevada university received so much national attention was that the events occurring at UN were not very different from the faculty-administration struggles going on at many other campuses during the 1950s.[38]

Although the charges against faculty members varied across campuses and included everything from insubordination, being uncooperative with the administration, Communist sympathies, and invoking the Fifth Amendment, all of the cases, at their core, dealt with academic freedom. Sheila Slaughter, a professor of higher education at the University of Arizona at Tucson, succinctly describes the situation at UN in her study of what she calls "dirty little cases" of infringement on academic freedom.

> In dirty little cases, administrators have usually treated faculty members like employees rather than professionals. They have charged faculty members who wanted to participate in institutional decision making with "insubordination," troublemaking," even "sedition." As the AAUP investigating committee remarked in one case, the reasons given by administrators for dismissals were "more appropriate to a military organization or an industrial enterprise than to an institution of higher learning."

According to the *New York Times,* "The [Richardson] case has had national repercussions as involving principles of academic freedom and tenure [by] testing whether a professor may be dismissed for opposing the administration on matters of educational policy."[39]

As a result of the efforts of the Friends of the University, the first petitions and letters began arriving during the last week in April and the first week in May. Petitions were received from the University of California faculty, the Stanford University chapter of the AAUP, and the University of Illinois, the latter initiated by Arthur E. Bestor Jr., the author of the controversial article. Bestor's petition from the University of Illinois, mailed to Silas Ross and the Board of Regents, was signed by thirty-eight faculty members and excoriated Stout's actions.

> We the undersigned are alarmed by the threat to academic freedom and tenure which appears to be involved in the efforts of President Minard W. Stout to secure the dismissal of Professor Frank Richardson, chairman of the Department of Biology. We . . . believe that certain

> principles set forth publicly by President Stout in his statement of the case are utterly untenable, and we are convinced that should these principles be made the basis for dismissing Professor Richardson, irreparable damage would be done to the University of Nevada.

According to the local newspapers, "more than 200 faculty members at University of California signed resolutions deploring [the] action of the Nevada university administration in the early phases of the dispute," while the Stanford University chapter of the AAUP found the "grave situation" at UN in need of "immediate investigation and appropriate action by the national office." In response to the letter-writing campaign mounted by the Friends of the University, Stout and the regents were bombarded with letters, telegrams, and other documents from more than twenty campuses carrying expressions ranging from indignation to dispassionate requests for more information.[40]

The regents and Stout chose to publicly ignore the many letters and petitions of support for Richardson, while proadministration Nevada newspaper editors loudly lamented the unwarranted interference by "outsiders." For those editors, just as for the administration and board, the issue at UN was a simple, straightforward case of insubordination; the problem involved an employee disobeying a boss, and it had nothing to do with academic freedom. One editorial in particular must have affirmed President Stout's self-assurance; it accused "these outsiders" of wrongheadedness because they expressed "support and sympathy for the Nevada faculty dissidents, and criticism of the officials who took action *through proper channels* on matters concerning purely Nevada university subjects." Two days later, the same newspaper printed a response written by Edda Houghton, a former educator from Wellesley College and a member of the Friends of the University. She explained that the petitions needed to come from "outsiders" because "those in the best position both on campus and in the community to understand the issues find their jobs, their friendships, their professional futures jeopardized by open discussion." The very meaning and purpose of a university are destroyed if "the most extensively educated people are fit to speak above a whisper only in their fields of specialization, whereas the general public can talk freely about everything."[41] The editorial and Houghton's response summed up both sides of the argument but did nothing to bridge the issues.

Of the many concerns that surfaced in the United States during the traumatic 1950s, Communist infiltration of higher education, one of the most vociferous, made its presence felt in the Nevada controversy. It became an integral part of the overall scenario and remained an unpredictable factor throughout the proceedings. The "Red" issue crept subtly into various public conversations at opportune times and occasionally into regents' meetings, but it made a very dismal splash during the second day of the Richardson hearings. The fact that the Red specter was a continual presence overhanging governance debates followed the same pattern at UN that was then occurring at all institutes of higher learning where the alleged Red menace threatened. But in most instances, as with the Richardson case, Communism was merely the vehicle for resolving confrontations of another color. According to Lionel Lewis, an assistant professor of sociology on the Reno campus from 1961 to 1963 and later a professor of higher education at the State University of New York at Buffalo, "controversies between faculty and administrative authorities invariably did move beyond simple and paramount concerns about communism, loyalty, patriotism, and national security." In their efforts to build a case against a faculty member as a radical, administrators were more focused on public relations than on larger political or ideological considerations.[42]

In the Richardson case, as Lewis suggests, Communism came up only as an aside, almost as an afterthought or as an additional way to bolster the administration's case. The confession of an administration spokesman supports Lewis's contention that Communism was not the underlying focus of administrative action. After allusions to "pinkos" had been made on previous occasions, this spokesman admitted that the reason the university was bringing the action was "to get rid of the biologist as part of a drive to 'clean up a bad situation' of long standing allegedly resulting from attempts of a 'small dissatisfied minority' of the faculty to run the institution."[43] The purpose was to remove a challenge to administrative authority, not clean out Communists. The issue was raised only by those who wished to create a sensation; as a legitimate focal point, however, it was a topic that ultimately failed to engender hysteria in Nevada.

The first time anyone openly expressed concerns about Communism was on February 25, 1953, during a Nevada State Assembly Education Committee hearing called in response to continued complaints about unrest in the university community resulting from Stout's change of policies. On the agenda were several bills proposing changes in the laws governing the university and its regents. In attendance at the hearing were President Minard Stout and Board of Regents members Roy Hardy and Louis Lombardi, all anxious to defend the recent chain-of-command policies as well as protect their administrative turf. Their chief antagonist was an ambitious, young Republican assemblyman, Gary Adams, from Washoe County. He read a letter from an unidentified writer who claimed "he had been told by two members of the regents that the bills which would restrict regent authority had been inspired by a group of professors who 'would not take the oath of allegiance.'" The implication of the supposed regents' statement was that assemblymen were "fronting for" oath avoiders who were obviously tainted by Communism.[44]

Not to be outdone in the Red-scare department, Hardy's summation of one of the proposed laws that would allow the legislature to restrict the powers of the board was that it "would only create the type of confusion Joe Stalin would relish."[45] As is obvious, anti-Communism in Nevada, as in most areas of the United States, was a response to current national concerns. It showed no real understanding of either the Communist ideology or how it was applied in Stalinist Russia. But it made good copy in the local newspapers. In fact, the entire discussion about oath avoiders was probably the outgrowth of an overactive imagination. The Nevada Constitution, written in 1865 when loyalty to the Union was a paramount issue, requires that all teachers sign an oath of allegiance to the nation and the state before they are hired. Simply put, if anyone refuses to sign that oath, the only oath in effect in the early 1950s, that person does not teach in Nevada.

There were others in the meeting who took the Communist threat more seriously. Assemblyman Rodney Reynolds, who saw Communism lurking nearly everywhere, queried President Stout about any measures "being done on the Hill to screen the staff as to Communism." Stout, confident in his own abilities as an administrator and judge of character, assured the assembly that he himself always thoroughly checked the backgrounds of all employees before he hired them.[46] This was the first oblique reference to the need for UN to have an anti-Communist oath. But the major controversies over anti-Communist oaths then going on at the University of Washington and the University of California tended to keep oath discussions to a minimum in Nevada. The topic stayed dormant until late 1953; at the present, Stout and the regents had a more dangerous challenge to face: that of the legislature trying to usurp their authority. The administrators were eventually successful in their united front against the assembly's Education Committee, and the authority-restricting laws were left to die without being reported back to the floor of the assembly.

Given the public's perception of an overt connection between Communism and radicalism, it was obvious that the topic would again surface in connection with the pending dismissals of the five faculty members accused of being a "small dissatisfied minority." Although there is no known public accusation that any of these scholars were connected with Communism, this highly exploitable issue was not to be left to languish if it could be of benefit. Fred M. Anderson, a local physician, member of the alumni executive committee, friend of the three English professors, and future member of the Board of Regents, visited President Stout's office on the morning of April 6,

1953, shortly after the show-cause letters had been issued. When Anderson queried Stout about the grounds on which these tenured faculty were being terminated, he was told "that all 3 were 'Pinkos' to [Stout's] knowledge, although he could produce no proof of this." Robert Gorrell, too, remembers the specter of "Reducator" hanging over his head during this time. The attorneys for the three English faculty "persuaded us at once that if we went into that . . . hearing, we were just asking to be fired, . . . that they [the administration] were working on trying to make it look as if we were communist sympathizers or something."[47]

On April 10, 1953, the same day that the state supreme court issued the writ of prohibition, the *Reno Evening Gazette* ran an editorial headed "Academic Freedom." The editorial strongly supported the March 1953 anti-Communist statement issued by the Association of American Universities (AAU). The AAU, the organization that represents the administrations of many of the nation's leading graduate schools, went on record as favoring the dismissal of all teachers who were members of the Communist Party. In the AAU's opinion,

> [A] scholar must have integrity and independence. This renders impossible adherence to such a regime as that of Russia and its satellites. No person who accepts or advocates such principles and methods has any place in a university. Since present membership in the Communist Party requires the acceptance of these principles and methods, such membership extinguishes the right of a university position.

The *Gazette*'s editorial explained the AAU's statement to its local audience in the following way:

> No teacher or other faculty member can be tolerated in American schools or universities if he is a Communist or a disciple of the party line. This is not a matter of an individual's private belief. Allegiance to Communism bars freedom of thought; the Red is a cultist whose mind is closed, who is a non-believer in academic freedom. . . . The universities have the right and obligation, as their leaders declared, to weed out Reds on their staffs.

This editorial also ostensibly offered a slap at the House Un-American Activities Committee for not respecting the judgment and internal policing capabilities of universities. From the editorialist's perspective, universities have the ability and the right to clean their own house, and only if "they fail in this duty should congress intervene."[48] The direct implication was that if the universities do not remove all faculty tainted with a Communist brush, legitimately or not, then the university is failing in its trust. But given the editor's faith in the authoritative attitudes of the board and the president, there was no doubt that by removing these five dissidents, UN would have fulfilled its obligations.

The editorial in the *Gazette* followed the same line of reasoning as did many other pronouncements made by anti-Communists in various magazines and newspapers over the decade. An article written in 1951 by the well-known former Communist and FBI witness Louis Budenz is a case in point. He, as did the *Gazette* editorial, linked academic freedom and Communism; but for Budenz, the two ideologies complemented each other. His writings often called explicit attention to the danger of retaining Communists on college faculties. In his article "Do Colleges *Have* to Hire Red Professors?" Budenz says, "Uncover a red doing his stuff on a college faculty and a hue and cry is raised over 'academic freedom': as though these people had a God-given right to infect our children with their made-in-Moscow virus."[49] The confusion, misrepresentation, and lack of understanding about the relationship between academic freedom and Communism continued throughout the entire controversy. Given the prominence of the Communist issue in higher education across the nation at that time, as well as the subtle hints about the leanings of the five dissidents, the *Gazette* editorial no doubt wished to remind Nevada's Board of Regents of its responsibilities.

The fact that the attorney for the Board of Regents suddenly injected the issue of Communism into the Richardson hearing left reporters for the *Nevada State Journal* bewildered; their counterparts for the *Reno Evening Gazette* were only slightly less perplexed. The Board of Regents chose to disavow any responsibility for bringing up the issue. From all viewpoints, it seems that the maneuver was not only misguided, but also directed at the wrong individuals and ended up hurting the university and discomfiting the Board of Regents. The discussion went so lamely that the *New York Times,* a newspaper actively interested in covering the issue of Communists in education, gave it only brief mention in its extensive reporting of Richardson's hearing.[50]

On the second day of the hearing, May 25, 1953, before a packed crowd of students, faculty, interested citizens, journalists, and observers from various local AAUP chapters in the auditorium of the university's Thompson Education Building, the subject of Communism was suddenly introduced into the proceedings. Harlan L. Heward, special assistant attorney general and counsel for the board, "dragged in the red issue" (or perhaps red herring) during his examination of Thomas Little, one of the original five and the vice president of the local chapter of the AAUP. Of particular interest to Heward was the AAUP statement favoring Communist Party members being allowed to teach, passages of which he had "underlined in red peculiarly enough." After ascertaining that the local chapter had disavowed the portion of the statement that entitled Communist instructors to the protection of tenure rules, Heward persisted in challenging Little's personal convictions on allowing Communists to teach. Although admitting that it was a complex issue, Little disclosed that he agreed "with Senator Robert Taft, who has said he does not feel that Communist party membership, of itself, should be grounds for dismissal." Little went on to enunciate his own belief that if such a teacher "attempts to influence his students with Red philosophy and propaganda then he should be dismissed."[51]

Finally, with the realization that he was digging a deeper hole for his case, the exasperated Heward made probably the biggest blunder of his examination of the Red issue. In a gruff voice he asked Little, "Well, are you a Communist?" Little responded that he was not only not a Communist, but a Republican and had "Q" clearance from the Atomic Energy Commission and the FBI for work at the atomic proving grounds in southern Nevada. The existence of Little's grant and its attendant clearance procedures had been common knowledge since mid-April, so for Heward to pose such a ludicrous question was proof to his audience that he had merely been attempting to smear both the AAUP and Richardson who was the president of the local chapter. The lack of success of Heward's probe into Communism was evidently exasperating for the Board of Regents, too. According to Gorrell, as Little was testifying, he kept responding to each of Heward's questions by referring to documents that he kept in his pockets. Toward the end of Little's interrogation, as he again removed a document from his pocket, one of the regents leaned over to a fellow regent and whispered in a voice that was overheard by almost everyone, "All these assholes keep notes!"[52] Naturally, the burst of laughter from the audience, already amused by the lack of success of Heward's line of questioning, did not help the prosecution prove Communist infiltration.

Local Reno newspapers reported that they did not know why Heward had chosen to focus on Communism, and, although he "dwelt on the Communist issue for about half an hour," he "did not publicly announce the purpose of his questioning." The *New York Times,* however, wrote that "Mr. Heward, out of the hearing room explained he had brought in the communist issue because 'serving as an officer of an organization [AAUP] with the stupid policy it shows toward communism, a policy it has reaffirmed, militates against [Richardson's] fitness as a teacher.' The attorney said he had no intention of trying to link Dr. Richardson with communism."[53] Heward's statement again begs the question because Richardson's fitness to teach was not part of the charges lodged in the bill of particulars. As some have conjectured, if the regents had already made up their minds to fire Richardson, then the attorney's entire venture into the realm of Communist influence on campus was directed toward convincing the public that the regents' decision was unquestionably correct.

Furthermore, Heward's disclaimer is refuted by Alice Terry, secretary to the president and the Board of Regents.

> One of the reasons that the regents didn't present a stronger case, so I was told by one of the regents himself, was that Mr. Heward thought perhaps there had been a Communist strain in the incident. . . . He immediately wanted to investigate the possibility of Communist influence. The regents were sure that there was no such thing. And they didn't even want it pursued. Mr. Ross mentioned in one of the later meetings that he felt that that weakened the regents' position.[54]

Terry's testimony supports studies that show that secondary pressures and conflicts as well as external political sources within a state could and did direct the course of the cold war on campuses throughout the nation.[55] If the Board of Regents believed strongly that there was no Communist conspiracy involved in Richardson's actions, then they should have had the right to direct their attorney away from that line of questioning. Such an action would be appropriate, especially in light of the seemingly disastrous results of Heward's efforts. However, because Heward was a special assistant attorney general for the state, he seemed to command a power that the regents could not, or would not, challenge.

Despite Terry's disclaimer about the Board of Regents's reluctance to make a connection among Communism, the AAUP, and the dissidents, there remains some question about who was really pushing the issue. Although Terry is sure that Heward was the one who believed there might be a connection, Frank McCulloch, editor of the *Nevada State News,* was not so certain. In the editorial he wrote after witnessing the Richardson hearing, he related that on the day prior to Thomas Little's testimony, during the testimony of someone else, one of the regents was reading a copy of *American Mercury,* a popular magazine with a resolute anti-Communist bias. Although McCulloch found the lack of attention disturbing, what he really found "to be an amazing coincidence" was "that the issue of *American Mercury* [the regent] was reading was one in which the AAUP was criticized for its 1948 resolution on the Communist question." In particular, McCulloch pointed out that the three major points against the AAUP made in the article were also the three points Heward attempted to make in his cross-examination of Little. McCulloch then raised the preeminent question of "whether the judge and jury—which the regents are in this case—were coaching the prosecutor or the prosecutor was coaching them."[56]

Although McCulloch was surprised at both the inattention of the regent and the presence of the *American Mercury* article during the hearing, others were well aware that the article in question was probably going to figure prominently during the cross-examination of some of the faculty witnesses, especially those who were members of the AAUP. In a May 4, 1953, letter to AAUP associate secretary George Pope Shannon, Richardson's attorney, Leslie Gray, stated that the regents had "circulated and marked copies" of the May 1953 issue of *American Mercury* that contained an article by anti-Communist fanatic J. B. Matthews. In the article, "Communism and the Colleges," Matthews sought to prove that the AAUP was soft on Communism by taking a single statement from the AAUP's 1947 report out of context and labeling it as "infused with unbelievable ignorance." By doing so, Matthews was able to claim that the AAUP was "made up of many misguided or fellow traveling educators." A second letter concerning the Matthews article was sent to Shannon on May 18, by Helen Wittenberg, secretary of the Friends of the University and wife of one of Richardson's attorneys. Shannon's response to both Gray and Wittenberg was to send copies of the five resolutions endorsed by the 1953 annual meeting of the AAUP and copies of the 1947 Committee A on Academic Freedom and Tenure report from which the *American Mercury* quotation was extracted.[57]

Shannon, in a May 20 follow-up letter, informed Gray that during a three-hour meeting the day before with Stout, general secretary Ralph Himstead, and staff associate Warren Middleton, he had been assured by the president that "he would use his personal influence with the regents of the university and with the Attorney General to prevent the introduction of this false issue [Communism] in the hearing." Stout said, however, that although he personally did not believe so, he was afraid that others might regard Richardson's presidency of the Nevada chapter of the AAUP with disfavor, especially in connection with the article by Matthews in *American Mercury* that had been widely read in the community. Shannon went on to advise Gray not to bring up the topic of Communism or to say anything that might give Attorney General William T. Matthews any cause to bring up the topic.[58]

Himstead himself reminded President Stout of his commitment to trying to keep the false issue of Communism out of the Richardson hearing and asked him to telegraph back whether the issue of Communism was to be introduced by the regents, the counsel for the regents, or any other representative of the administration at the university at the hearing on May 25. The

AAUP, according to Himstead, needed the information to determine if they should send an observer to the hearing. Stout did not respond, the AAUP's central office did not send an observer, and the issue of Communism was introduced at the hearing.[59]

In examining the events surrounding the "small dissident group," it is obvious that the Communist issue came up only in response to specific challenges to the authority of the administrators. It first showed in the regents' response to the Nevada State Assembly Education Committee's attempted takeover of board powers; it later flickered in Stout's response to Dr. Fred Anderson's challenging query about charges against the dissidents; and finally, its most flagrant appearance was in the hearing itself, where the public was witness to Richardson's active defiance of the autocratic governing structure of the administration. Therefore, Communism, at least on the Nevada campus, came to symbolize not the horrific destroyer of American liberty, virtue, and democracy, but the deflector of attacks on the autocratic power structure of the Board of Regents and the fire wall against challenges to President Stout's chain-of-command ideology.

The subsequent dismissal of Frank Richardson, as a result of the regents' decision in early June, reflected negatively on the university, its administration, and the board itself. Much was made of the fact that during the hearing, the regents, who had been involved in filing the initial charges and had hired the prosecuting attorneys, sat as judge, jury, and executioner. Obviously, no system of checks and balances was allowed to operate on the UN campus. But it was their steadfast insistence on maintaining as their sole right the exercise of control over decision making that brought the most grief to the board over the next five years. Through their chosen representative, President Minard Stout, the regents were able to exercise power at the expense of ever restive issues of academic freedom and faculty participation in governance. Had the predicament at UN been ignored outside the state, it would have resolved itself only very slowly over many decades. But because these same issues were being contested on large and small campuses around the country, the controversy at UN became part of the overall picture, and its outcome was subject to the same influences that were assailing the others.[60]

2: Who Is the Boss, Anyway?

"'Almost any moron can get into college,' bewails an eminent educator. Yes, and what's more deplorable, he can also get out of college, taking a degree with him." So wrote humorist and sage Olin Miller in his daily vignette on the editorial page of the June 11, 1953, issue of the *Reno Evening Gazette.* This amusing anecdote was printed next to editor John Sanford's commentary that championed the Board of Regents's decision to dismiss Professor Frank Richardson. The juxtaposition of these two pieces is ironic because Richardson was dismissed for challenging President Stout's plans for lowering admission standards to the university. One wonders if Sanford, a staunch conservative and loyal backer of board chairman Silas Ross, saw any irony in this placement.[1]

Many in the Reno community, if they even noticed the irony, did not find it humorous. Frank Richardson was astounded at his dismissal and called the regents' decision to fire him "a mockery of justice." One of his attorneys, Bruce Thompson, was even more blunt. "I'm flabbergasted. I don't see how five men could get so far off the track." Novelist Walter Van Tilberg Clark, renowned author of *The Oxbow Incident* and *Track of the Cat* and lecturer in the UN English department, sent his letter of resignation to department chairman Robert Gorrell. In that June 1 letter, he expressed his fears that the administrative situation at UN would only get worse, and that although he had intended to await the verdict of the hearing, he believed that the regents had decided to fire the biology professor even before the hearing began. In a convoluted single sentence, Clark elaborated on his decision.

> Now, having witnessed the greater part of those proceedings, and being unable to read into the regents' abrupt termination of them, or into the delay in announcing their findings until after the inauguration of the president, anything except a preconceived intention, whatever they have in store for Dr. Richardson, not only to condone, but to perpetuate and implement that autocratic administration and thus, tacitly, also to approve the several acts of personal discrimination in matters of position, salary and tenure which I know to have occurred under it, as well as the unwarranted and damaging affronts to yourself, Dr. Richardson, and three other members of the faculty which led to the hearing, I cannot but feel that the decision has practically been forced upon me.

The *Nevada State News* wondered if firing Richardson was an attempt to quench "controversial fires which have been raging for weeks on and off the campus [and if it was, had the regents] doused the flames with water or fuel."[2]

Fuel, it seems, turned out to be the liquid of choice of the Board of Regents. Shortly after the board disregarded overwhelming testimony on the biologist's behalf and voted for dismissal, Richardson's attorneys, Bruce Thompson, Ralph Wittenberg, Bert Goldwater, and Leslie Gray, petitioned the Nevada Supreme Court to examine the evidence to determine if it was sufficient to warrant that decision. On June 19, the high court issued a writ of certiorari in response to the request by Richardson's lawyers. This move in itself caused another major ripple in the ongoing trauma at UN and to some extent in the state as a whole. Because a writ of certiorari is an order from a higher court to a lower one requesting the record of a case for review, the implication is that the state high court viewed the actions of the regents as if they were a court presiding over a case. The attorneys for the administration filed a motion to quash the writ of certiorari, contending that the supreme court could not hear the appeal because the state constitution gave the regents "exclusive administrative and executive power over the affairs of the university." Therefore, they contended, a high court review would be unconstitutional because the Board of Regents had acted as an executive board, not as a judicial one. Because the state constitution provides for separation of powers, the judicial branch cannot sit in judgment of the executive branch.[3]

As long as the regents were acting within the scope of their jurisdiction, which includes the right to hire and fire faculty members, they could not be controlled, supervised, or countermanded by the supreme court. But it was the very issue of jurisdiction that Richardson's attorneys were calling into question. They contended that the regents had exceeded their jurisdiction and authority because the original bill of particulars stated no legal cause for removal, the testimony during the hearing established no legal cause for dismissal, and "no witness testified and no evidence was produced showing that [Richardson] had not been cooperative."[4] The supreme court, by virtue of refusing to vacate the writ of certiorari as petitioned by the board's counsel, in effect proclaimed that the Board of Regents, in this instance at least, had acted as a court of judgment and therefore its decision was subject to review. This somewhat contrived intrusion of the judicial branch into the executive branch not only threatened the autonomy of the Board of Regents but also set a possible legal precedent for future cases.

Much of the board's argument in their December 23, 1953, "Respondent's Brief" requesting the dismissal of the writ of certiorari was based on the United States Supreme Court's decision in *The National Labor Relations*

Board, Petitioner, v. Local Union No. 1229 in early December 1953. The gist of that decision was that "there is no more elemental cause for discharge of an employee than disloyalty to his employer." The case that occasioned the Supreme Court decision involved a suit by employees who were fired for distributing pamphlets. The justices determined that the firings were justified because the "company's letter [of dismissal] shows that it interpreted the handbill as a demonstration of such detrimental disloyalty as to provide 'cause' for its refusal to continue in its employee [*sic*] the perpetrators of the attack." Although the board's attorneys admitted that they had paraphrased the court ruling, they maintained that the Bestor article was "a demonstration of such detrimental disloyalty as to provide 'cause' for their [the regents'] refusal to continue in their employ the perpetrator of the attack." Furthermore, it did not matter what reason Richardson gave for distributing the article; the interpretation of whether the article itself was detrimental was entirely within the jurisdiction of the board.[5] The attorneys also reminded the Nevada high court that the term *cause* has no legal definition, thus implying that if the regents believed they had cause to fire Richardson, then their obligations had been legally fulfilled.

By keeping an employer-employee relationship in the forefront of their argument, the administration hoped to bolster their support among the naturally conservative, hierarchy-oriented sector of the citizenry. Toward that end, regent Archie Grant, who owned the Ford dealership in Las Vegas, was not reluctant to say, "A university professor was no different than a Ford mechanic; he had to obey his boss." The inherent conservatism within the state and especially that of many newspaper editors, which had been evident from the beginning of the troubles, grew more obvious after the regents' dismissal decision and during the debates before the state supreme court. However, there were many in Nevada who were struggling to move the state into the mainstream of a rapidly progressing twentieth century. This group felt that decisions such as that made by the regents were based on traditional conservatism and would forever doom Nevada to remain the "backwater" the rest of the nation had labeled it. Furthermore, they resented the popularization of such views as later presented by Ed Reid and Ovid Demaris in their 1963 sensationalized best-selling exposé, *The Green Felt Jungle.* The authors gave no credence to the surging forces for change in Nevada that were struggling to break free of the traditional past, writing, "Except for a few irascible natives, no one takes the state of Nevada seriously."[6]

The dismissal of Richardson with its inherent overtones of "fired disloyal employee" sparked a sharp exchange between the *Las Vegas Review-Journal* and Bruce Thompson, a Richardson attorney and former member of the

Friends of the University. In an editorial, pointedly titled "Showdown," the *Las Vegas Review-Journal* wrote, in direct response to the dismissal hearing just ended, that although the affair was unfortunate, it had, indeed, served a purpose. That purpose was to put the faculty on notice that any attempts to use academic freedom as a way to set up some sort of "super-government" of their own were bound to fail. In language similar to that of Louis Budenz, the editorial implied that academic freedom is in the same realm that patriotism was for Samuel Johnson, the last refuge of a scoundrel. But the writer took his argument one step further by asserting that academic freedom "has been one of the vehicles upon which the pinkos have ridden into places of eminence in universities all over the land." Although the editorial disclaimed knowledge of any "wide-to-the-lefters" on the Nevada faculty, its addendum that, "to our knowledge, there are few if any disloyal instructors in the institution" left open the door for continued suspicion of any faculty member who might choose to defend academic freedom. Again alluding to the nationwide rampage against Communism in higher education, the editorial reminded its readers that Communists' use of academic freedom to infiltrate the system "has been done in other educational institutions throughout America and it could happen here."[7] The implication was that faculty members, especially leftists, were apt to use the device of academic freedom to insert themselves into the governance structure of an institution. Once there, they would be in a position to usurp power from the rightful authority and destroy the sanctity of American education. Therefore, Stout and the regents had done the right thing to stop a potential threat and protect UN from the hands of leftists.

Taking umbrage at the editorial's charges against academic freedom, attorney Bruce Thompson responded to the *Review-Journal*'s article in a letter to the *Reno Evening Gazette*, which had reprinted the Las Vegas editorial. Thompson cogently summed up his argument, as well as his contempt for the editorial writer, in one sentence: "Those who speak of communism and academic freedom in one breath understand neither." Thompson emphasized that "one is the antithesis of the other. . . . [C]ommunism is . . . based upon strict regimentation and control of schools, newspapers, libraries and all forms and processes of teaching and instruction—while academic freedom is to schools what freedom of the press is to newspapers and freedom of assemblage to persons interested in public affairs."[8]

Thompson was not alone in his rejection of the administration's attempt to cloak issues of academic freedom in the narrow terms of boss versus worker. Many students, too, were deeply involved in the issue and resented what they believed were Stout's dictatorial attitudes toward both themselves and the faculty. Stout's suppression of faculty and student input into the governance of their institution was diametrically opposed to the ideology and principles of individuality inherent in a university education. Even Sidney Hook, a disciple of the John Dewey school of pragmatism and an adherent, like Stout, to the belief that it is an individual's right to obtain the education that would permit maximum growth and that it is society's duty to provide it, opposed the elimination of faculty participation in governance. "Not only on good educational grounds, but on prudential ones as well, the administration must draw the faculty into the formulation of institutional educational policy." He believed it was prudential because if the president alienated the faculty by denying them participation, in instances where he needed their support he would find them either neutral or, as Stout discovered, hostile.[9]

In his "Pack Tracks" column in the student newspaper, the *U of N Sagebrush,* Rollan Melton wrote in Richardson's defense: "Freedom of the press and freedom of speech boil down to the same thing. . . . They are separated only by a semicolon. If Dr. Frank Richardson is guilty, then his sin has been allegiance to academic freedom. And without that freedom, how can educators seek out the truth and pass it on to each succeeding generation?"[10] In 1950s Nevada, in loco parentis, like extreme conservatism, was beginning to give way to postwar modernity and progress.

The growing population center of Las Vegas approached the boss-worker issue less dogmatically because its two newspapers held differing opinions on how a university should be run. The *Las Vegas Review-Journal,* every bit as conservative and patriotic as rural Nevada newspapers, favored autocratic control by the Board of Regents and the president. "The University of Nevada is [a] big and important business. It should be run on a business-like basis and the board of regents should have full and complete control of the curriculum, the entrance requirements and the entire operation of the institution. The faculty is the hired help and cannot, in the interests of harmony, have any hand in the administration of the institution." The editorial further insisted that neither seniority, tenure, nor academic freedom gives an employee the right to question the boss's orders. This editorial echoed its Elko counterpart that argued the regents must take charge or succumb to being merely figureheads. The *Review-Journal*'s antithesis, the *Las Vegas Sun,* drawing on an editorial by Frank McCulloch of the *Nevada State News,* took the position that for the university to condone character assassination for the sole purpose of winning Richardson's dismissal "hardly fits the American concept of justice." The *Sun*'s editor, Hank Greenspun, was taken to task by one of his fellow editors for espousing the "neopink" line about "rights." Evidently, Greenspun's belief that "if all the brains of the country are to be regimented into one line of thinking, there will be no necessity to try and contain the Communistic philosophy" did not fit with the rural editor's idea of "how things ought to be run in our little old democracy."[11]

Outside of Nevada, the press reports in the major newspapers that carried the story generally supported the faculty's right of academic free speech and academic freedom. A *New York Times* article cogently summed up the controversy between the contestants in Nevada. It reported that the president and Board of Regents's viewpoint was that the hearing would "determine whether the university will be run by its administration or by a group of 'authority usurpers' within the faculty." The faculty perspective was that the hearing would "show whether faculty members may be thrown out for daring to express opinions on educational policy opposed to those held by the president and the regents." Each of these points of view is a direct reflection of the diametric nature of the interpretations of employer-employee and administration-faculty relationships. Robert M. MacIver, professor emeritus of political philosophy and sociology at Columbia University, has studied this dichotomy. He states that academic freedom cannot survive in an environment of misconceptions such as "the notion that the educator is a hired man who can and should be told by his employer how to do his job, a notion that is still entertained by some of the more unregenerate governing boards."[12]

The boss-worker relationship was also intrinsic to Stout's personal definition of tenure: "[T]enure is a privilege conferred by the president on a faculty member which can be revoked at any time." Although his definition did not accord exactly with that of the Board of Regents's policy, in the long run the end result was almost synonymous. The regents' own statement of the tenure policy provides that a faculty member with tenure can be dismissed only for cause and after a hearing. The tenure statement had been published as recently as February 13, 1950, in "Faculty Bulletin no. 37" that specifically stated that the "provisions [were] adopted by the Board of Regents on January 24, 1948, and amended on May 26, 1948."[13] The board's lawyers, Attorney General William T. Matthews, Special Assistant Lester D. Summerfield, and Special Assistant Harlan L. Heward, in their brief submitted to the Nevada Supreme Court in December, made the point that the regents had followed their guidelines. They had held a hearing for Richardson and found what they believed was cause for his dismissal.

This point, however, was incidental because, as the attorneys went on to say, "We contend that this tenure rule is not binding upon the regents but that in their executive capacity they may ignore the rule if they so see fit." That is to say, rules binding on employees are not necessarily binding on the employer. The issue of who was bound by the rules of tenure turned into a useful point of contention to draw public attention back to the boss-worker controversy. To substantiate the claim that the Board of Regents did not have to abide by its own rules, Heward pointed out that most administrative bodies operate under that same principle, but generally they all try to follow the rules closely whenever feasible. Richardson's attorneys were quick to decry the "obviously immoral implications" inherent in such a stand because, they pointed out, "if the regulation is not binding on the regents, it is binding on no one." Under such conditions, the regents' guarantee of tenure "becomes mere empty words constituting a fraudulent misrepresentation by the governing board of the university to all who accept or retain faculty employment here expecting the benefits of tenure as partial compensation for services rendered."[14] Indeed, if the Board of Regents has the sole power to hire and fire faculty, and if their own tenure rule is not binding on them, then who is bound by it, and is it, ultimately, of any value at all? This important question was only one of several the academic community wanted addressed by the Nevada Supreme Court; another was the administration's attack on academic freedom.

While the supreme court ground its way through the evidence from the Richardson hearing, other issues were evolving, and these too revolved around President Minard Stout and the Board of Regents. One such issue was the spreading dissatisfaction among the faculty at UN and the dissemination of that discontent to the rest of the country. In his June 1 resignation letter, Walter Van Tilberg Clark blasted Stout for perpetuating an "increasingly autocratic administrative attitude" in an effort to create a "faculty of manageable mediocrity." These remarks were brought to the attention of the nation by both *Time* magazine and the *New York Times*. The regents' response to Clark's declaration was that because he was appointed on only a temporary contract, he had no position from which to resign. Regent Newton Crumley believed that the publication of Clark's resignation letter was "deliberately done for a malicious purpose."[15] The regents' rebuttal, however, was not given the same national coverage as Clark's accusations.

The same publicity scenario occurred when Professor Thomas Little submitted his resignation. The letter in its entirety was printed in the *Nevada State News* with excerpts printed in the two Reno newspapers and in the *New York Times*. In his July 11, 1953, letter, Little, one of the original defendants and the object of Special Assistant Attorney General Heward's Red-scare tactics, cited an "alarming curtailment of freedom of speech on the university campus, [caused by] the unhealthy concept of an efficient administration through rigid adherence to a chain of command [where] the president and the regents must prove that they are 'boss' instead of . . . leaders." Little also cited the existence of pay-raise favoritism as he alluded to the potential for development of Nazism's milder form: "Stoutism."[16]

With Little's departure from UN, his Atomic Energy Commission grant to study the effects of atomic-bomb emissions upon plant life was discontinued. At the end of July, President Stout received a letter from the AEC director of biology and medicine stating that because the research project had been built around Little, his resignation from the university caused the plans to be dropped. However, the influence of the administration and the regents in Nevada politics was made clear when Senator George W. (Molly) Malone wrote a letter to the chairman of the AEC urging him "to expedite appointment of a man to head up the research program at the university." The seemingly inexhaustible supply of money being invested in atom-related research, the university's close proximity to the Atomic Proving Grounds in southern Nevada, and the avid interest of the state's national politicians all coalesced to reduce the financial effects of the loss of Little's grant; new projects were soon made available. President Stout announced in early December that the university was granted nearly twenty thousand dollars by the AEC to do research on the livestock industry.[17]

During this time, several other aspects of Stout's leadership style were made visible to the public: the creation of new schools and the construction of new buildings were two facets that seemed initially to be a boon to the university and the state. Upon closer examination, though, these structural changes caused some to question how ethical and justifiable, or even necessary, it was to establish these programs. One of the first major changes in the structure of the university proposed by Stout and approved by the regents was to move the School of Education out of the College of Arts and Science and create a new College of Education. Stout reminded the regents that the Nevada Constitution had specifically included teacher training as one of the necessary components of the state's educational program.[18] When the state no longer supported normal schools, the training of teachers fell to the university. Initially, there had been a College of Education, but in 1937, due to budget constraints, it was abolished and incorporated into the College of Arts and Science. By the 1950s, as the school-age population of Nevada exploded in the postwar boom, the shortage of teachers became acute. Locally trained teachers who would work within the state school systems were the ideal solution, and increasing the status, scope, and curricula of the school at UN was the way to attract students and satisfy the state's need for teachers.

Consequently, Stout obtained the unanimous approval of the Board of Regents for the 1954 fall semester reestablishment of the College of Education that was to have "the status of other Colleges on the Campus, [and] to give the College of Education the proper leadership, it should be headed by a Dean." Given the already ambiguous attitude toward Stout and his fellow educational bureaucrats, as well as the continuing, though subdued, controversy over the lowered admission requirements, this move was particularly fraught with contention on campus. Stout's insistence that the new college would "tighten up" the existing curriculum, which contained sparsely attended, unnecessary, and overlapping courses, seems to be in opposition to reports by other sources. The new college, according to a *Nevada State News* report, would offer a full schedule of one-, two-, and four-year courses, both B.A. and B.S.; graduate degrees; study in teaching and administration on elementary and high school levels; Saturday, evening, and off-campus courses; study for teaching in both urban and rural schools; as well as specialized courses such as kindergarten, art, and music. To many this seemed more of an expansion than a tightening. According to Alice Terry, the contention over the College of Education was further aggravated when Stout, after conducting a search in the same manner as the one through which he was chosen, that is, the job seeks the man, hired Garold Holstine, a close friend whom he had known prior to coming to Nevada, to head the new college. It may be of no little consequence that of the seventeen criteria for the position of dean presented to the regents by Stout, the last was "[i]magination, initiative and courage."[19]

Many at the university and throughout the community, including regents Archie Grant and Louis Lombardi, believed that Harold Brown, current director of the School of Education, should have been promoted to the deanship. But the two regents backed down after Stout "assured them that . . . Brown had been given 'due consideration.'" Regardless of Stout's testimony, it had not been forgotten that Brown had impeded the president's case against Richardson. The *Reno Evening Gazette* reported, "The claim has been made that the deanship was created in the first place to grease the skids for removing Brown from the faculty because he gave aid and comfort to Richardson." Reminding the regents of their promise that he could pick his own lieutenants, Stout had no trouble successfully gaining their approval for Holstine's appointment.[20]

After the creation of the College of Education, there came the expansion of the School of Home Economics and its new building named for Sarah Hamilton Fleischmann. In 1956, Stout opened the College of Business Administration in the newly built Silas E. Ross Hall named for the by-then retired chairman of the Board of Regents. The final burst of growth, attributable to Stout's administration, was the Orvis School of Nursing in 1957.[21] Stout and the regents believed they were responding to the state's future educational needs by constructing colleges and schools to fit the trends of the 1950s. It was their insular decision making about what schools to promote and which contractors to hire, however, that became a focal point of contention.

An incident that also reflects Stout's status with the regents was his acquisition of a new presidential residence. After the board approved his recommendation for the Fleischmann home-economics building, he used its construction as a pretext to get the regents to purchase a house for him off campus. As the plans for the construction of the home-economics building progressed, the contractor naturally cleared the blueprints with Stout. The building, however, soon outgrew the initially planned land allotment, causing a section of it to encroach upon the back of the president's on-campus house. Upon inquiry, the contractor explained that the offending section was to be the training area for the students to learn how to direct children's play. Stout replied, "Kids! I don't want any kids in my backyard! I've raised my children." The next day, Stout called the contractor and said, "Your plans gave me an idea. I'll prevail upon the Board of Regents to sell the house and buy me a house off campus. That's where it should be because they treat all presidents on campus like they own your kitchen, borrowing pots and pans, and that sort of thing! Something like they do for a rector in a church."[22] Stout's acumen at convincing the regents that his status required more respect was evident because shortly thereafter, they purchased a "mansion" on Mount Rose Street that then became the presidential home for many years.

While Stout was obtaining the board's approval for the College of Education, the necessity of hiring additional faculty to staff it, as well as increasing staffing needs in general, caused some to question why UN had no safeguards against the infiltration of "Reducators." Hence, the decision to implement an anti-Communist oath, although seeming to arise suddenly in October 1953, was a direct response to public concern about left-leaning academics. The new statement would be an additional oath to be signed by everyone and would in no way displace the loyalty oath already required by the state constitution. The University of Nevada regents, unlike those of most of the institutions Lionel Lewis studied in *Cold War on Campus,* did not focus their rhetoric on the need to keep Communists off the faculty. The Nevada regents publicly stated (and the resultant anti-Communist statement confirmed) that the main reason for instituting a statement was to reassure the public. But the ultimate goals of the UN administration were the same as those Lewis found concealed behind the imposition of oaths in most other institutions: the need to maintain institutional stability and the concentration of power in the hands of administration. By requiring the signing of an oath or statement, administrations were able to "hold their positions, vis-à-vis faculty and over time.

Principals who cooperated were publicly acknowledging that they recognized who ultimately controlled the college or university." That the maintenance of the power structure within the university system was, indeed, the focus of administration was made obvious during the California oath controversy. Even though the University of California regents all agreed that the faculty members who refused to sign the required oath were not Communists, they decided by a vote of twelve to ten to insist upon discipline and fire all thirty-one. A study of the situation at California found that "[t]o refuse to sign was to be disobedient, to flout the board's authority, to desire to substitute one's own judgement as to standards of employment to resist the discipline of the University over its employees."[23] Thus, by firing the nonsigners, the California regents were able to keep their power structure intact and to intimidate any future challengers.

It is evident that UN's administration, too, was more concerned with maintenance of power than with eliminating "Reducators." Alice Terry, secretary to the president and the regents, remembers that Communism was not an overriding concern with the regents, especially with Chairman Silas Ross. In his oral history, Ross makes little reference to Communism in higher education, except to mention that "Dr. Stout was against it." That Stout was against Communists in higher education cannot be doubted. In early 1953, he, along with presidents of numerous other institutions, requested from Lewis W. Jones, president of Rutgers University, a copy of "Academic Freedom and Civil Responsibility." This popular document was Jones's definitive statement concerning the validity of academics taking the Fifth Amendment when testifying before a duly constituted governmental body. Jones stated that "for members of a university faculty to refuse to give a rational account of their position on vital community matters" seriously damages the university's best defense against the attacks on it and "in fact cuts the ground out from academic freedom itself."[24] This document, had the need arisen at Nevada, provided Stout with the strong support of an eminent president from a prestigious university that had already gone through the trauma of a congressional investigation. As the case turned out, however, the Fifth Amendment issue never arose at UN.

Although fully prepared to use the document against any faculty member who might invoke the Fifth Amendment, Stout completely overlooked the assertion in Jones's statement that the "minimum responsibility" of members of the university was to "state frankly where they stand on matters of . . . deep public concern, and of . . . relevance to academic integrity."[25] This is exactly what Richardson did in his attempt to state where he stood on the issue of lower entrance requirements. In the long run, then, it is obvious that

Richardson was not punished for refusing to speak out, or even for speaking out, but for refusing to shut up.

With all the clamor about Communism that had surfaced during the Richardson hearing, and the media coverage of HUAC investigations of "Reducators" nationwide, it would have been surprising if some sort of anti-Communist oath was not developed for UN. But regent Newton Crumley's introduction of the issue of an oath during the October 13–14, 1953, board meeting seems to have caught Chairman Ross and others by surprise. Ross credits Crumley with introducing the resolution "[t]hat knowing a member of the Communist party is not free to teach the truth, the regents will not appoint a member of the Communist party to the faculty." The only reason for Crumley bringing up the topic that Ross can think of is, "Well, we had a faculty member who was a Russian teacher and he was quite active—he was a scholar. Well, he was the main one, and frankly, it was sensed a little bit in other departments, but there was none as active as this fellow was. The regents thought that the sooner that we expressed ourselves on it, the better." That faculty member was Anatole G. Mazour, a Russian historian and a soldier in the czar's army during World War I, and as such was a White Russian to whom Communism was anathema. Mazour taught at UN from 1938 to 1947 and later transferred to Stanford University.[26] The lapse of six years between when Mazour left and Crumley introduced the oath issue was never explained and probably accounted for the surprise of its introduction.

However, the issue of Communism on campus had come up in the Nevada State Assembly Education Committee meeting in February 1953. Of course, it noticeably arose during the Richardson hearing and was a consistent item in the press. But whatever the reason, the *Reno Evening Gazette* reported that the issue again arose at the regents' October meeting that was dedicated to the presentation of personnel recommendations. After the recommendations had been approved, Crumley asked President Stout "if all of the faculty recommendations had been screened as to their political beliefs [which he later defined] as referring to Communists." Even though Stout assured the regents that he "was of the opinion none of them had Communistic beliefs," Crumley pursued the discussion of the need for an oath or statement because he thought "it is very important. It is done in other universities."[27]

According to the minutes of the meeting, after the Crumley statement was adopted, the board then instructed the president "to submit a recommendation on the mechanics of achieving this objective." The account of the meeting as reported in the *Nevada State Journal* reminded the public about the regents' recent discomfiture during the exploration of the Communist angle in the Richardson hearing. "The university governing board approached the problem of Communists in education with surprising suddenness and then handled it in gingerly fashion." In fact, when reporters queried whether Nevada would require a "loyalty oath" like those that had recently caused controversy at the University of California and the University of Washington, among other institutions, they were told that the regents were "not thinking in terms of an oath. . . . Applicants would merely be asked the question." The regents also told reporters, Chairman Ross's earlier statement notwithstanding, that they were confident that the present faculty was free of Communists.[28]

The Board of Regents and the president took a lesson from the University of California's struggles to implement a non-Communist oath in 1949–1950. First, they did not call their creation an "oath," thus eliminating any overt questioning of the faculty's veracity. Second, President Stout worked through committees to create the statement rather than forcing on the faculty a statement created by "outsiders." Third, signing the statement was made voluntary rather than mandatory. Fourth, the statement applied to staff, faculty, and administrators then working at or through the university and, therefore, did not single out faculty. Fifth, the statement did not require disclosure of previous affiliations, thus eliminating concerns about past misjudgments. Although some of these items were still contentious among faculty members, the president and the regents tried to make the statement as palatable as possible. Indeed, the statement soon came to be called the "Quaker Oath," because it merely required its signer to "affirm," not swear.[29]

The text of the non-Communist statement was the end result of collaboration among various factions at the university itself. The local newspapers reported that the final wording was agreed upon through meetings of many committees, including the newly created thirteen-member faculty advisory committee, two general faculty meetings, and meetings of secretarial, building and grounds, and clerical workers. One faculty member recalls, however, that the committees that helped design the statement were "loaded with deans and administrative yes men." But President Stout emphasized that agreement and volunteerism were the hallmarks of this effort. He specifically pointed out that the faculty had agreed on three main points: "that the so-called Communist party cannot be considered a political party [a slap at the AAUP]; that there is concern among the people about any possible infiltration of faculties [a sop to outside political pressure]; and that it would be better for the university to be in the position of 'using its own broom' than to have any other group move in that direction."[30] The latter reference was obviously directed toward the ongoing HUAC and McCarthy-committee investigations that were wrecking havoc on campuses across the country.

However, Robert Gorrell, one of the original five dissidents, remembers that the process of creating the non-Communist statement was not as harmonious as Stout implied. He recalls that the faculty was very much concerned about having an oath forced on them. In light of their recent experience with repression at the hands of the administration, and especially since the appeal hearing of the Richardson dismissal was about to begin, many believed that the statement was "obviously intended to be used as a club." Despite the potential threat inherent in the situation, some faculty members protested, "since we had decided in advance that this was a ploy to try to get something on some people so that they could be dismissed later." But Gorrell corroborated Stout's statement that the wording was a communal effort, although the amity of the discussions differed between the two points of view. According to Gorrell, faculty meetings were held to "get the oath watered down so that it wasn't too obnoxious" even if it remained discriminatory.[31]

If any harmony existed among the conferring groups, it was lost on Professor Everett Harris. He recalls, "In the fall of 1953, Stout and the regents made all members of the University staff sign a statement that they did not belong to the Communist Party." He further questions the necessity of such a statement, especially in light of the regents' October statement that they believed the faculty to be free of Communists. Harris and Gorrell both hit upon a major problem that administrators faced in attempts to institute oaths at other universities and colleges: discrimination. Harris asks, "Why were University professors singled out for this treatment among all the employees of the state of Nevada? Why weren't public school teachers, highway department employees, etc., asked to sign a similar statement?"[32] Although Harris overlooked the fact that all university employees were asked to sign the statement, he was correct that other State of Nevada employees were not.

Even though nonuniversity personnel were not required to sign an oath, the state legislature did not overlook the possibility of Communist influence in state government or public education. During the 1955 legislative session, Assemblyman Gary Adams introduced two bills that addressed the state's fears about Communism. Assembly Bill AB 43 imposed the "duty upon public employees" to answer questions concerning their beliefs in the "forceful and violent overthrow of the government of the United States or of any state, membership in organizations advocating forceful or violent overthrow of such governments" on penalty of termination if they failed to do so. Assembly Bill 44 provided that the "advocacy by a public employee or a public school teacher to overthrow the United States Government or of the state by force, violence or other unlawful means or membership by a public employee or public school teacher in an organization advocating overthrow of such governments by force, violence or other unlawful means, to be sufficient cause for dismissal." Although AB 43 died in the assembly Judiciary Committee, AB 44 was passed by both houses and signed by Governor Russell on March 1, 1955.[33] It made up for what the Quaker Oath lacked: it required disclosure of membership in the Communist Party and made that sufficient cause for dismissal.

Furthermore, there is a slight difference between Harris's and Stout's interpretations of the obligation to sign the statement. Harris states that the faculty were made to sign the statement; Stout's position was that everyone would be asked to sign the statement voluntarily and that there was no deadline for signing. However, he went on to add that if anyone refused to sign the non-Communist statement, the case would be examined by the Board of Regents before the issuance of the next contract.[34] The difference, then, between Harris's point of view and that of Stout is only a matter of degree.

The non-Communist statements were distributed to the university faculty and staff on November 6. By December 8, President Stout, in preparation for reporting to the Board of Regents meeting on December 10, proclaimed that "the faculty is cooperating wholeheartedly with the administration in accomplishing the purposes of the statement and many faculty members had signed the statement voluntarily." The regents themselves voluntarily signed the anti-Communist statement on December 9. But after the December 10 meeting, the two Reno newspapers, in revealing the fissures in the docility as earlier presented by Stout, also revealed the split biases within the community. Although neither paper put the article on page 1, their respective story headlines reflected their perspectives. The December 11 issue of the *Reno Evening Gazette* announced in a two-column head, "Faculty Members Sign Statements," and that same day the *Nevada State Journal* in a bolder three-column head shouted, "Only One Instructor Fails to Deny Commie Tie-Up." Edwin Bayley, a key political reporter in the McCarthy era, reminds us that "[s]tudents of the press have long been in agreement that the headline is the most important element of a news story, serving both as an index for the reader who is 'shopping' the paper and as an ultimate, concentrated digest of the news story."[35]

During the board meeting, Stout told the regents that the "cooperation and attitude of faculty members in solving the Communist statement problem was [*sic*] excellent. 'It could have been dynamite, if someone had grabbed the ball and attempted to fight it.'" That Stout's praise of faculty cooperation and attitude was window dressing was pointed out in several faculty oral histories. Although many signed because they genuinely believed it was the appropriate thing to do, some signed because they were demoralized and afraid of recriminations; they did not want to give the administration any reason to "cause a fuss" again.[36]

The one faculty member who refused to sign was accorded very little attention in the media. Even the *Journal,* whose bold headline decried the lone holdout, only mentioned that the regents did not discuss the case of the unidentified instructor. The only media support the recalcitrant received was in an editorial in the *U of N Sagebrush,* the student newspaper. The editorial commended the English instructor, Howard Houston, for refusing to be pressured into signing a "ridiculous" statement that was worthless because it was not even notarized. The student author believed, "The instructor is well rid of a position with a university which allows itself to become tinged with the shame of 'witch-hunting!'" Houston, by refusing to sign the statement, made himself a victim of the times. According to history professor Ellen Schrecker, during the early 1950s, the academic community was "accommodating itself to some of the most discreditable aspects of McCarthyism. Not only had it agreed to exclude from its ranks those people, i.e. Communists, whom it had defined as unqualified, but it was becoming willing to sacrifice as well people who, though never accused of being Communists, were unwilling to submit to a political test and prove that they were not."[37]

That the anti-Communist statement presented to the existing faculty was more in the nature of a formality was made even more obvious when the president and the board released the requirements for new applicants. In addition to signing the existing statement, anyone applying for a new position with the university would be asked three questions, the two that reflected the applicants present affiliations plus the ubiquitous and deadly, "Have you ever been a member of the Communist Party?"[38] This questionnaire for new hires was intended to screen out all academic Communists. Because the questionnaire contained the statement that "the Regents will not appoint a member of the Communist Party to the faculty," any applicant who was a member of that organization had two options: not to sign or to lie. However, because conventional wisdom held that Communists were not trustworthy, then it would be a safe assumption that those applicants would lie and therefore the statement was worthless, just as the *U of N Sagebrush* editor had noted.

President Stout, in "Faculty Bulletin no. 410" dated January 13, 1954, attempted to bolster the administration's case for requiring an anti-Communist statement. Attached to the bulletin was a copy of "The Land-Grant Colleges and Universities and the Principle of Freedom," a document distributed by the Association of Land-Grant Colleges and Universities that clarified the organization's stand on academic freedom and Communism. This statement, like those of both the Association of American Universities and UN, advocated the removal of "any member of the Communist party or any one subject to its disciplines." Further, the statement, like that of Rutgers president Lewis W. Jones, regarded "candor in response to official inquiry as a proper test of competence to conduct teaching, research and public service in these publicly supported programs of activity." Of secondary, or perhaps primary, importance to Stout, however, may have been the section on the organization's insistence upon "due process and legal safeguards versus popular pressure and unproved accusation in their appraisal of staff integrity."[39] Perhaps he hoped that if the faculty realized that he and UN were in compliance with the dictates of the land-grant association on issues of Communist infiltration, and were in the mainstream of current educational policy, then they would also accept the fact that he was within his rights on the Richardson issue. But under any circumstances, by early 1954, the Communist issue on the Nevada campus seems to have been solved or was at least ignored until the late 1960s and the protests against the war in Vietnam.

On April 20, 1954, the Nevada Supreme Court reversed the regents' decision to terminate Professor Richardson, and as a consequence he was reinstated to the university faculty. President Stout, in this instance, publicly practiced what he preached. In his public statement, he said, "All my life I've worked for someone else. I have adjusted my pattern of operation to higher authority. If a higher authority overrules me, that's it." The *Reno Evening Gazette* presented the story in a single column with an understated head and subhead: "Regent Lawyers Accept Verdict in Faculty Case: Richardson Ruling Part and Parcel of Our Government." The *Nevada State Journal,* however, reported the entire story with a five-column head and two-column subhead that declared: "Supreme Court Unanimously Finds Regents Had No Legal Basis for Firing Richardson: Pres. Stout Bows to Authority; Ross Declines to Comment."[40] The *Gazette* presented the matter as though it were an unremarkable occurrence within the normal functions of a democracy, thus limiting the negative reflection on the administration and the Board of Regents. The *Journal,* on the other hand, implied that because the ruling was based on "legalities," the board and Stout had broken the law by firing Richardson. The fact that Stout unquestioningly accepted the court's ruling as an inherent part of the "chain-of-command" principle reinforced the president's original stand against Richardson. Although Stout did not publicly denigrate the court's decision, many conservatives throughout the state who strongly supported the hierarchical business approach to management were frustrated at the supreme court's interference with the popularly elected Board of Regents. Their cause was amply taken up in editorials in rural newspapers that decried the usurpation of the board's independence as most unpatriotic.

Much of this frustration was expressed in the opinions of small-town newspaper editors. For example, the *Elko Independent* wrote that just when the question had been solved by the regents exercising their law-given right to fire Richardson, the Nevada Supreme Court intruded and reopened a closed case. "Now comes the state supreme court and sets itself up to judge whether the regents had sufficient evidence against Dr. Richardson to justify their action. . . . Is the supreme court attempting to decide an administrative matter or is there some question of law involved?" A year later, the patriotism of autocracy was still as strong as ever. In mid-1954, just after Richardson was ordered reinstated, the *Elko Independent* ran the following baleful, if somewhat overstated and quixotic, condemnation of the disregard for the "American way of life."

> Incidentally, did you ever see a group of men elected by the people to do a job who had less to say about that job than the board of regents of the university? If it isn't the legislature telling them how to run the university it's the supreme court and if it isn't the high court putting in two-bits worth it's the governor.
>
> It seems to me that the regents ought to stand up on their hind legs and tell the world they are going to run the university—let the legislature cut off their funds, let the supreme court overrule them and let the governor hamstring them but "by Godfrey, we're going to run the university!" should be their battle cry.

These sentiments were not limited to rural Nevada. A letter to the editor in the *Gazette* presented a local Reno resident's positive but myopic view of absolutism: "Let's face it, we elect the board so right or wrong in our eyes let them do as they see fit."[41]

As can be expected, however, Professor Richardson's reinstatement did not resolve the problems facing UN during the 1950s; in fact, in many ways it exacerbated them. In May 1954, economics professor Arthur L. Grey Jr., perhaps emboldened by the recent court decision, wrote a scathing letter of resignation reminiscent of those written by Walter Van Tilberg Clark and Thomas Little a year earlier. In it, Grey complained of Stout's autocracy and that despite the president's concern for democracy in educational opportunities for students, he had no such scruples about democracy for faculty. According to Grey, "[T]he men who spoke for a principle were felt to have no place in a regime which recognizes expediency as its master." He further stated, "[T]he university is in full retreat from the observance of the fundamentals of democratic behavior."[42] Nor did coming back to Nevada solve Richardson's own problems: he was shunned by the administration and suffered threats and challenges from anonymous sources within the institution.

The year between his dismissal in June 1953 and his return in August 1954, Frank Richardson took advantage of a fellowship grant offered him by Yale University to conduct research through the Bernice P. Bishop Museum in Hawaii. His work there culminated in a treatise on the dark-rumped petrel, a rare and little-studied bird native to the Pacific islands. The notoriety and respect accorded him by his successful association with Yale were soon augmented by the citation he received from the Committee on Education of the American Civil Liberties Union. In November 1954, Richardson received a citation from this committee because he "refused to abandon the rights of a teacher to discuss educational policy, despite warning from the administration and loss of his job until restored by the Supreme Court of Nevada."[43] The public accolades for Richardson did not reflect well on the university administrators who had fired him for being insubordinate and uncooperative. Nor did they do anything to ease the tension between him and Stout.

Upon his return to campus, he was reinstated to his teaching position, but not to his former role as department chairman. Because chairmanships were awarded on a year-to-year basis, and were held at the discretion of the president with the approval of the regents, that Richardson did not retain the biology chair was not surprising. Furthermore, the current holder of the chair, Ira LaRivers, had been a witness for the administration during the dismissal hearing. However, other changes in Richardson's status proved much more difficult to explain. Some faculty believed that because the Board of Regents and President Stout had been compelled to bring Richardson back, they were trying to find ways to force him to resign. His teaching schedule was untenable because he was assigned classes that were outside his expertise and denied classes he had previously taught. Furthermore, he was not assigned an office; he could hold office hours only because a friendly professor allowed Richardson to use half of his office.[44]

Not only was he subjected to the vagaries of scheduling, but he was also exposed to personal attacks. Strange materials, perhaps chopped rubber bands, were put in his smoking tobacco, and it was feared that someone might be trying to poison him. He was also the recipient of derogatory anonymous letters and notes, and on at least one occasion, his campus mail was opened and his signature forged. It was hinted that his faculty replacement and perhaps even the department chair were working with the administration to get him to leave because they were afraid he would attempt to reclaim his old jobs. How accurate these reminiscences are is unknown, but under any circumstances, neither the chairman of biology, the dean of Arts and Science, nor the president stepped in to help Richardson solve his problems. As a result, he took a leave of absence at the end of the spring semester in 1955, "driven out by the remaining bad feeling." He departed for a visiting lectureship in zoology at the University of Washington and later became the curator of birds at the Burke Museum at that same institution. There he continued a distinguished career that included the founding of the Washington Environmental Council and convincing the Nature Conservancy first to work to create the Skagit River Bald Eagle Natural Area and later to acquire more than a half-dozen islands in the Puget Sound archipelago as natural avian sanctuaries. In recognition of his singular efforts to protect the habitat of rare bird species, much as he had earlier fought for academic freedom, a preserve in the Puget Sound islands was named in his honor.[45]

Even before Richardson came back to campus, however, the need for an investigation of the university was being discussed. A January 9, 1954, proposal by Assemblyman Gary Adams called for a three-pronged investigation by a nine-member interim committee. The committee would investigate the low morale of the staff at the university, the confusion surrounding the pending sale of the university farm, and the inadequacy of insurance coverage on university-owned buildings. The proposal was defeated, but it was only one of several indications that a legislative investigation was becoming a distinct possibility. In a letter dated January 16, 1954, student Barbara Jean Brown broached just that subject with Governor Charles Russell. Students, she wrote, in addition to suffering the stigma of the university's tarnished image because of its treatment of Professor Richardson and suffering the deprivation of the "excellent instruction of such men as Dr. Tom Little and Mr. Walter Clark" who left because of unfair treatment of faculty, were now being subjected to an "atmosphere of intimidation and discrimination." The student's primary complaints were a reduction in class offerings that deprived students of needed classes and the increase in faculty loads that deprived the students of the best efforts of an overworked faculty. The implication was that the faculty who resigned in response to the administration's authoritarian practices were not being replaced, and as a result, the students' educations were being neglected and the university's reputation was being destroyed. In addition, an anonymous letter written to the state legislature at the beginning of its 1955 session purported to list the "Facts—supporting the idea that an investigation should be conducted at the University of Nevada by the State Legislature."[46] The letter cataloged in detail all the alleged past sins of Stout and the board. Although the letter purported objectivity, it was obviously slanted against the administration.

The final impetus for an investigation came from Allvar H. Jacobson, an associate professor of sociology, who was distraught over the "inhuman and capricious treatment [of faculty] which seems to be Dr. Stout's stock in trade." In a February 16, 1955, letter addressed to Chairman Ross, he also expressed "'disgust' with Professor Richardson's 'trial,' and condemned Dr. Stout for discrimination against those members of the faculty who had supported Professor Richardson." He further stated that Stout's tactics were "unbearable," that Stout did not trust his subordinates, and that he was an "unprincipled administrator" whose continuation as president would be "disastrous to the University." Jacobson copied his letter of complaint to the regents, the governor, and key members of the state legislature, including Gary Adams. Arts and Science dean Fredrick Wood called a meeting of departmental chairmen at which they voted nearly unanimously not to offer a contract to Jacobson for the coming year; Charlton Laird recalls that Professors J. Craig Sheppard, Robert Griffin, and Maurice Beesley abstained from voting.[47]

Jacobson was called before a special executive session of the Board of Regents on March 5, 1955, to defend his charges. In testimony taken later by the AAUP investigating committee, it was pointed out that in attendance at the special session were Jacobson, the five regents, Attorney General Harvey Dickerson, an attorney who appeared as a friend of Jacobson, three state assemblymen, a student reporter for the *U of N Sagebrush,* the Alumni Association president, as well as newspaper, radio, and television reporters. Professor Charles H. Monson Jr., then president of the Nevada AAUP chapter, requested to have a faculty member or representative of the AAUP attend the session, but his request was denied by the Board of Regents. In response to much close questioning by the regents and the attorney general during the morning session, Jacobson defended his charges. At the afternoon session, the deans appeared and expressed their confidence in Stout's administration.[48]

Because of the seriousness of Jacobson's charges, or perhaps the breadth of the circulation of his charges, the legislature believed it could no longer avoid addressing the question of an investigation. Speaker of the assembly Cyril Bastian, a recipient of Jacobson's letter, asked "several assemblymen to find out if an agency exists that can study the institution from top to bottom." He further stated that he would vote for an appropriation to fund such an independent study. Stout, again demonstrating the techniques of an "organization man," backed the proposal for an independent probe of the university. However, his sense of self-assurance led him to interpret an independent investigation from an entirely different angle. In a public statement that reaffirmed his confidence and corroborated the correctness of his chain-of-command philosophy, he stated:

> I consider it immediately imperative to the welfare of this university and its students that an inquiry be conducted into all phases of my administration by an impartial board of nationally recognized men qualified to evaluate the programs of land grant colleges.
>
> This university cannot continue to function effectively in the face of destructive letters such as this, letters filled with innuendo and accusation and very little fact.
>
> If there are those who challenge my administration let them publicly present their arguments and back them up with facts. I stand on my record as president. In the last two years I feel this university has made splendid progress.[49]

But Stout was not the only person singled out for criticism; the Board of Regents bore the brunt of another letter to the governor. This letter, dated February 28, 1955, and signed only as "A member of the teaching staff, 'on tenure,'" queried Governor Russell on the possibility of changing membership on the Board of Regents from elective to appointive. It suggested that the governor was naturally the best possible person to appoint competent regents who would have the best interests of the university at heart. In two responses to E. Allan Davis dated April 9, 1956, and November 12, 1957, Governor Russell endorsed the idea of appointing members of the Board of Regents. "I have always held that the Regents should be appointed in this way, and in this way there would be a closer relationship with the State government. The men named should not be politicians, but should have the good of the University in mind." In addition, in his opening address to the 1957 session of the Nevada state legislature, he made reference to having advocated regent appointment as early as 1955. "I recommend as I did two years ago, that the offices of the Regents should be appointive instead of elective, which will necessitate an amendment to the Constitution of Nevada."[50]

As the pressure kept mounting, the legislature, on March 23, 1955, finally ordered and funded an independent appraisal of the university. The objectives of the consultants, according to the statute, were to make "an investigation into the administration of the University of Nevada and to report the results thereof and make recommendations in connection therewith to the legislative commission."[51]

The situation at UN had come full circle. Stout and the regents had forced the dismissal of Frank Richardson for "cause," namely, insubordination. But the state supreme court had ordered his reinstatement. The high court based its judgment on the fact that the board had overstepped its jurisdiction by disregarding its own tenure rules; it did not, however, rule on the issue of academic freedom. Much to the disappointment of many in academic circles and in society at large, the court's failure to do so seemed a vindication of Stout and the board's governance policies. Armed with the backing of the court, then, Stout was sanguine about an investigation because he believed that it would corroborate his personal administrative ideology, as well as mollify his detractors. He and the board continued their policies and were so confident in their control that they eagerly recommended organizations to participate in the upcoming study. Their insular focus, however, kept them from recognizing the hardening of attitudes then occurring among the students and faculty on campus and within the community itself. By 1956, they would see the error of their ways.

President Minard W. Stout, 1953. Courtesy 1953 *Artemisia,* Dan Loveless, editor.

Biology professor Frank Richardson, 1941. Courtesy University Archives, University of Nevada, Reno.

1954 Department of English. *Left to right, row 1:* Paul Eldridge and Jeanne Lawson. *Row 2:* Robert Griffin, William Miller, Charlton Laird, and Robert Gorrell. *Row 3:* John Morrison and Robert Hume. Courtesy 1954 *Artemisia,* Dick Morrill, editor.

1955 Department of Biology. *Left to right:* Fred Ryser, Ira LaRivers, Donald Cooney, Lowell Jones, Frank Richardson, and Robert Miller. Courtesy 1955 *Artemisia,* Janet Van Valey, editor.

1956 Board of Regents. *Left to right:* Bruce Thompson, Louis Lombardi, board secretary Alice Terry, Chairman Silas Ross, Archie Grant, and Roy Hardy. Courtesy 1956 *Artemisia,* Evalyn Titus, editor.

President Minard W. Stout, 1957. Courtesy 1957 *Artemisia,* Myram Borders, editor.

3: Let the Investigations Begin

"America has no academic freedom. There is no freedom of speech in America," said a Communist in Eastern Europe to Anatole Mazour. "Ah, now we know about America. What about Nevada? What about 'Stoot!'?" Thus had President Minard Stout's attack on academic freedom at the University of Nevada become a cause célébre in many parts of the world and for many reasons. In fact, Professor Robert Gorrell remembers that while making speeches in various Australian cities while on a Fulbright teaching fellowship, he was asked questions about Nevada and the Stout affair, no matter what the topic of his lecture.[1] But for Stout and the Board of Regents, it was business as usual on the hill.

Business as usual, in this instance, meant that things were happening at a fairly rapid rate and often in diametric directions. The disclosure of the contents of Professor Allvar Jacobson's letter to the heads of state and the Board of Regents created reactions in all quarters of the campus and the legislature. In addition to the board's executive session hearing, Cyril Bastian's investigative committee efforts, and the deans' vote of confidence, the president of the Associated Students, Clair Earl, after polling the students at Bastian's request, sent a letter to the Speaker seconding Jacobson's call for an investigation, and the students of all campus dorms met to decide whether to endorse an investigation. Even President Stout, after receiving his unanimous vote of confidence, urged an "immediate investigation by an independent agency."[2]

The editor of the *Reno Evening Gazette* believed, as undoubtedly did the president and regents Silas Ross, Roy Hardy, Archie Grant, and Louis Lombardi, that Jacobson's attack was encouraged by those members of the local community who were unhappy that an investigation had not been called after the Richardson fiasco. The editor named no names, but it is apparent that he believed that the Friends of the University had been involved in encouraging an investigation. The editorial pointed out that the 1954 election for regents showed that there was no great popular demand for a legislative investigation and, as well, proved that the "popular indignation about alleged wrongs on the campus was imaginary." During that election, regent Newton Crumley had decided to run for a seat in the Nevada state senate and regent Louis Lombardi's four-year term had expired. The editorial found the election unremarkable because Lombardi easily won reelection, even though there were eight other candidates in the race; each professed varying degrees of dissatisfaction with the previous actions of the board. Bruce Thompson, a former Richardson attorney, was elected to fill Crumley's seat. The editorial also made negative references to the campaign propaganda disseminated on Thompson's behalf. Although the authors of much of the campaign material remained anonymous, the content and the rhetoric matched those of the letters sent to other university personnel during the Richardson controversy in 1953.[3] These documents were sent by the Friends of the University, the group to which Thompson had belonged prior to his representing Richardson at the dismissal hearing and before the Nevada Supreme Court.

After hearing Jacobson's justification of his grievances against President Stout at the meeting on March 5, 1955, the regents decided to support the call for a probe of the university. However, the reasons voiced by the four original regents created the impression that a probe would "clear the stains" from the Stout administration and vindicate the previous actions of the board. Only regent Bruce Thompson implied that an investigation would show that the president was the cause of the problems and that the regents had been derelict in their duty. Another reason, unvoiced but of primary importance, to insist on an investigation was to be found in the radiogram dated March 11, 1955, that Chairman Ross received from Arthur E. Orvis. Orvis was a prolific donor of funds whose active interest in the university's status and its future was evident in the public congratulations he sent to Stout and the board for firing Richardson in 1953. Jacobson's charges being more scurrilous, Orvis's message this time implied that his continued support of the regents and Stout would not translate into continued financial patronage if the Jacobson controversy were not properly addressed. The message read, "Unfounded charges by unscrupulous individuals are damaging university prestige. As a donor of over $110,000 to University of Nevada and planning to give more I call for disciplinary action against Jacobson and others of his ilk. President Stout has my unstinted endorsement and esteem. Please give this message the fullest possible publicity." The intervention of Orvis into the fray demonstrates one source of external pressure on institutional governance. According to scholars in the field of higher education, one of the primary oversight responsibilities of a board of regents is the preservation of institutional independence. Boards of regents often face the difficult task of attempting to accomplish what they believe is best for the university without offending special-interest groups, especially those who can exert pressure by providing or withholding substantial financial support.[4]

Fear of the loss of institutional prestige, reputation, and, consequently, private financial support, according to scholars such as Lionel Lewis and Neil Hamilton, often compels administrators to take action against faculty members.[5] In Nevada, however, the Board of Regents was not concerned that Jacobson's attack would damage the university's prestige and reputation. They had supported Stout's earlier actions and would continue to support his administration because they firmly believed his approach was correct. The regents were fully aware, however, that to allow an affront such as Jacobson's to go uncontradicted would adversely influence donors and possibly restrict the donation of private funds and encourage more faculty protests. Consequently, though the viewpoints of Ross and Orvis were probably not very far apart concerning Jacobson, the fact that a primary donor was demanding action may well have strengthened the chairman's determination to solve the problem quickly and efficiently.

The extent to which the majority of regents felt justified in their cause was indicated by their instructing newly elected attorney general Harvey Dickerson to contact three nationally recognized organizations "for the purpose of selecting the ultimate investigating group." The regents and Stout believed that these three groups, the American Council on Education, the Association of Land-Grant Colleges and Universities, and the National Association of State Universities, should participate in the selection of the investigative group because many of these associations' leaders held similar administrative philosophies. Evidence of this similarity is indicated by President Stout's nomination to a senate committee of the Association of Land-Grant Colleges and Universities later that same week. That the president and the board's actions would be vindicated was also championed by an editorial in the *Nevada State Journal.* The writer summed up his argument by stating, "An inquiry into University of Nevada affairs by a competent group from one of the agencies mentioned may clear the air provided the investigating agency can find something more than trivialities to investigate."[6]

During the course of the regents' discussions about the need for the probe, the discrepancy between the points of view of regent Thompson and the others centered on the veracity of Jacobson's testimony. Regent Archie Grant, taking exception to Jacobson's statements that "his attitude toward Stout was 'the same as that toward Hitler and Stalin,'" requested that the deans of the colleges be called to present their views of President Stout's administration. His motion was supported by Chairman Ross and regents Louis Lombardi and Roy Hardy, who, in addition, questioned Jacobson's mental stability. Only Thompson voted against calling in the deans on the grounds that "the internal affairs of the University were as Jacobson described them." He indicated that calling the deans to give public testimony would be harmful to the university; perhaps he believed that such public testimony would cause the deans more trauma than had the anonymity of a private vote of confidence. The deans, nonetheless, were called to testify, and, not surprisingly, all of them found Stout to be professional, respected, extremely capable and qualified, above the average of his predecessors, forthright, energetic, and not dictatorial. Thompson, again in the minority, brought to the board's attention an interview he had had with C. B. Hutchinson, recently retired dean of the College of Agriculture. In that interview, Hutchinson had stated that "Stout wanted to make Nevada a 'teacher training school.'" Thompson went on to add that "since Stout has been here, there has been dissension and turmoil. This then would pose the possibility that there might be something wrong with the internal administration of the university."[7]

Because Jacobson's letter and testimony had attacked both President Stout and the Board of Regents, and because the deans had boldly and publicly disavowed Jacobson's charges against Stout, Archie Grant felt compelled to attest for the board. In a statement that affirmed the deans' testimony and did the board one better, he vouched that there were "no dictators around here, neither the president nor the Board Chairman Silas Ross." It was a "good board to work with," and there was no intimidation. Grant was quickly supported by Roy Hardy who declared that "Chairman Ross had 'given almost his complete life to the university and had served most honorably and nobly.'"[8] The public confirmation of selfless devotion to the welfare of his charges fitted perfectly the image of the grand patriarch that many attributed to Ross.

In an effort to further inspire the legislature to empower an investigation, petitions were sent to Speaker Bastian by UN students and by townspeople. One petition, signed by "607 students," requested an impartial investigation "in view of existing conditions and the confusion that exists on the campus." It and a second petition with even more signatures were turned over to Assemblyman Gary Adams as head of the search committee. At about that same time, the University of Nevada alumni executive committee was also encouraging the legislature to fund an investigation. At a meeting on March 14, 1955, attended by alumni, assemblymen, senators, the attorney general, Louis Lombardi, and other interested persons, the alumni executive committee placed strong emphasis on the need for the probe to be both impartial and thorough. Regent Lombardi and Senator and former regent Newton Crumley agreed heartily; Crumley even telephoned Governor J. Bracken Lee of Utah to inquire about the cost and procedures of two similar investigations of the University of Utah and Utah State College.[9]

The alumni, after listening to Attorney General Dickerson present probe recommendations from the regents' list of educational organizations, including the U.S. Department of Health, Education, and Welfare, introduced their own list. From the viewpoint of the alumni, organizations recommended by the board and evaluated by the board's attorney might not guarantee an independent investigative committee. Consequently, Dr. Fred Anderson, turning the focus away from the idea of an investigative group or body, submitted a list of individuals who might help make the investigation more objective.[10] The *Reno Evening Gazette*'s earlier editorial claiming a lack of public interest notwithstanding, it seemed that many local groups wanted to actively participate in an investigation of the university's administration, and to determine whether, as Allvar Jacobson had claimed, the continuation of Stout's policies would be "disastrous" to the university.

The regents evidently believed that they had the situation under control and that the outcome of the investigation was a foregone conclusion. Regent Lombardi asserted that the results of such an investigative report would be "extremely valuable in determining future policies of the university." He further promised that "the board would do its best to carry out recommendations by the investigating group." Senator Crumley went Lombardi one better and in a burst of enthusiastic ardor declared, "I have complete confidence in the board to follow the report of the investigating group, even if it will mean the resignation of every member of the board." Easy for him to say. In the end, it was decided that the short amount of time remaining in the 1955 legislative session necessitated that the search be turned over to a legislative commission. The Nevada Senate, on the last day of the 1955 session, introduced Senate Bill (SB) 270 to require an investigation, the price tag of which required an appropriation of twenty-five thousand dollars. The bill was introduced on the last official day of the legislative session, March 17, 1955. That does not mean that it was pushed through both houses in one day. As is the practice of the Nevada state legislature, when midnight of the sixtieth and last day of the official session arrives, the legislators merely stop recording the date and time their sessions. Consequently, SB 270 and all other legislation addressed on the sixtieth day, March 17, 1955, through the final adjournment were listed in the Nevada Senate's and Assembly's *Journals* as having been transacted on that last date. In actuality, SB 270 was passed in the state senate by a vote of twelve to zero, with five absent, including Senator Crumley. The bill was forwarded to the assembly, where it was approved by the Ways and Means Committee, amended by Assemblymen Rodney Reynolds and Gary Adams to investigate not only the administration but also the "academic operation," and passed by a vote of thirty-seven to three, with two abstentions. SB 270 was then returned to the state senate where it was approved as amended, and sent to Governor Charles H. Russell on March 22, 1955, who signed it on March 28.[11]

The investigation proposal and the appropriation bill were not without their detractors, however. Some legislative skeptics were only assuaged by the regents' assurances that they would abide by the report's findings. Others, echoing the earlier sentiments of the *Elko Independent* and expressing the true spirit of western autonomy, held that outsiders had no right meddling in the business of the state and the university. Assemblyman Don Crawford, a Democrat from Washoe County, stated that "the legislative counsel bureau was capable of conducting the study," and he added, "if we need new regents and a new president at the university, let the voters decide."[12]

While the legislative commission was proceeding with its task of locating a competent, objective investigative group, President Minard Stout made himself the focus of public attention. On April 2, two events took place that, although they may have been intended to improve Stout's image and standing with the community, the national educational organizations, and the potential investigative committee, merely exacerbated his relationship with the faculty and their supporters. At the behest of the regents, at least of Ross, Grant, Lombardi, and Hardy, President Stout was given "tenure at the rank of full professor in the university community." The measure was passed after much "tense but quiet" discussion, which saw Hardy strongly supporting tenure because otherwise the president was serving on a "day to day basis." On the other hand, Thompson strongly opposed granting tenure because he was afraid that such action might "tie the hands of future boards in the matter of administration."[13] Furthermore, he did not believe that it was a proper business relationship between a university and its president. Although Thompson made no reference to Jacobson's charge that Stout's continued administration would be disastrous for the university, his concern was based on his goal of getting rid of the president. By holding tenure as a professor, even if Stout were fired as president, he could still claim a position as a professor in the College of Education.

The second event was initiated by Stout himself. Given the trauma and dissension occurring on campus, in the community, and elsewhere in the country over his stance on academic freedom and faculty participation in governance, Stout decided to reorganize the faculty. In a reported effort to "provide opportunity for members to voice criticism," Stout set up four procedures for faculty members to air their grievances. Each of the four, naturally enough, followed the chain-of-command technique that one finds in many business environments and lay at the heart of Stout's administrative philosophy. The aggrieved party could go to his department head, with the right to appeal to the dean of the college, the president, and the Board of Regents; one of the twenty-two standing committees on campus; faculty meetings of his college, which were to be held once a month in the future; or, last, a special faculty commission that was to be elected by the faculty to hear complaints (or, as Stout termed them, "gripes").[14]

The viability of these grievance-resolution procedures was questionable at best. An example of the creation of the faculty committees gives evidence as to their sanctity. On several occasions, when faculty were asked to vote for members of committees, Stout collected the uncounted ballots and returned to his office. Before the committee needed to meet, various faculty members, including some very unpopular ones, would be notified by the president's office that they had been elected to serve on the committee.[15] Although this evidence did not conclusively prove that the elections were rigged or that the members would be more amenable to the president than the faculty, it did destroy faculty confidence in both the committee and its decisions.

In addition, the fall 1955 reinstatement of a university-wide monthly faculty meeting called the Faculty Forum turned out to be a perfunctory patch that did not service faculty interests at all. According to one faculty member who attended the forums, they were "to be held once a month for the purpose of discussion only, and I might add, guided discussion." Furthermore, in case anyone thought that the faculty once again had power within the governing structure of the university, the minutes of the December 13, 1955, meeting clarified the issue. The Committee on Voting Privileges, after long consultation with Academic Vice President and Stout appointee William Wood, clearly stated its decision that "[t]he Faculty Forum is not a legislative body."[16] But regardless of how or if Stout's new arrangements worked, these new committees and forums were in place and well publicized. Thus, the public was made aware that the administration was doing all that was practicable to accommodate a faculty that had, itself, been very unaccommodating.

Regardless of how earnestly Stout tried to mitigate the ongoing controversies, new conflicts continued to arise to focus attention away from his good works. In late April, Russell Kirk, author of the recently published book *Academic Freedom: An Essay in Definition,* made President Stout and the University of Nevada famous once again across the nation. In a letter to the *Nevada State Journal,* which he copied to the *New York Herald Tribune, Time,* the *Chicago Tribune,* the *New York Times, Newsweek, Reporter, Commonweal,* and columnist Walter Lippmann, Kirk claimed that the university librarian, James J. Hill, had removed his treatise from circulation and had torn up the records that showed the library ever owned it. Kirk, an eminent conservative in his own right, believed that the book was removed because it contained an extensive examination of the Richardson case and included criticism of Stout's "academic autocracy." Hill's response to Kirk's charge that "an arrant violation of free expression has been committed at the university" was quickly forthcoming. Hill stated, "Because of the extreme controversial nature of the book and due to the fact that it presents only one man's criticism, I decided to prepare a list of other titles on other points of academic freedom so that a balanced collection would be available for faculty and students." Hill said he purchased the library's only copy of *Academic Freedom* for his own library and ordered another copy to be placed on the shelves once a collection representing all aspects of academic freedom had been built.[17] Although libraries do not normally withhold titles until collections are complete, it is not an unheard-of procedure. It is neither unusual for books to be withdrawn from circulation without their authors ever being notified nor unusual for appraisal copies to never be shelved.

If, as some suspected, Hill had an unspecified agenda for removing the book, so too did the persons who notified Kirk. The obvious implication of Kirk's agenda was to imply that the librarian was pressured by Stout to remove the book, but Hill firmly asserted that he had acted on his own volition. An editorial in the *U of N Sagebrush,* the campus newspaper, suggested that Kirk possibly had another agenda besides the cause of academic freedom: getting his story in all the prominent newspapers and magazines would be a great advertisement for his book. Furthermore, the editor doubted that Stout had given Hill orders to remove the book because the president had already been involved in much unfavorable publicity, and, because the book was available in bookstores anyway, he would not unnecessarily risk more. The editor posited that if Hill were acting on his own, he was doing so not out of an "atmosphere of fear," as some might imply, but because he was trying "to do the administration a favor." Neither Kirk's information, obtained from "unidentified students," nor Hill's claim that the appraisal copy of the book had never "been placed on [or] removed from the shelves" can be proved.[18] Regardless of the circumstances, the heated controversy over Kirk's book was representative of not only the volatility of the tensions on the UN campus, but also how the issues of academic freedom quickly gained Nevada national attention.

Nonetheless, a copy of Kirk's book was reordered on April 25 and did go on the shelf shortly thereafter; it was first checked out on May 19, 1955. It appears that both Kirk, who feared students would not be allowed to read "the truth," and Hill, who was afraid that they would get only one perspective, overreacted to the potential impact of *Academic Freedom*. The circulation record indicates that, in addition to the May 19 date, the book was checked out once in 1956, once in 1965, once in 1966, twice in 1969, and once in 1973. Although this is not exclusive proof that not many read the book, the fact that only one store in town sold out its limited supply and the public library had a waiting list of only four people indicates that it did not become a best-seller.[19] As an indication of the incestuous nature of politics, personality, and community, on the same page of the *U of N Sagebrush* as the article about *Academic Freedom*'s availability, there was an advertisement for the book at Gray Reid's book department; Assemblyman Gary Adams, who had been a thorn in Minard Stout's side from the very beginning, was a member of the family that owned that department store.

The library controversy had barely cooled when it was announced that Committee A on Academic Freedom and Tenure of the AAUP was going to conduct an investigation into accusations of the denial of academic freedom at UN. The AAUP had been monitoring the situation since April 2, 1953, when it first received notification from Professor Thomas Little. In addition to Little, requests for an investigation were made by Helen Wittenberg; Leslie Gray; the presidents of the AAUP chapters from the University of Illinois, the University of Alabama, San Diego State College, Fresno State College, and the University of Hawaii; as well as Joseph Robertson, I. J. Sandorf, and Russell Elliott of the Nevada chapter. In a response dated June 23, 1953, AAUP general secretary Ralph Himstead assured the Fresno State College chapter that the "situation will be thoroughly investigated." Himstead's letter was apparently sent to other chapters as well because on July 1, Russell Elliott, the secretary of the Nevada chapter, reported that the local executive committee had approved the move to investigate the Richardson case.[20]

True to his word, Himstead began organizing an investigative committee on July 16, 1953, when he telegraphed requests to Professor Robert B. Brode of the University of California at Berkeley to act as chairman and to Professor Eugene H. Wilson of the University of Colorado to be a member. Austin E. Hutcheson, a history professor at UN, also weighed in on the subject of members of the investigative committee. He strongly recommended against anyone from the University of California at Los Angeles, especially any political science professors. He suggested several names, including that of Anatole Mazour. One of his recommendations, Ralph Lutz of the Hoover Institute, had already been in contact with Himstead concerning the situation at UN, during which he referenced Stout's "canine ancestry."[21]

In view of the fact that Professor Richardson's dismissal was being adjudicated in the Nevada court system, the AAUP did not initiate its investigation. According to George Pope Shannon, AAUP assistant secretary, if the state supreme court upheld the termination and if Richardson formally requested an investigation, the AAUP would be "prepared to enter into a full investigation with a view to the possible publication of a report for the information of our members, the profession at large, and the public."[22] Richardson, writing from his Hawaiian research location, did make a formal request on October 21, 1953. But because the state supreme court had not yet rendered a decision, the investigation was put on hold.

To further complicate the matter, at the AAUP Council meeting in Washington, D.C., held in February 1954, Shannon, in his "Statement to the Council, Relative to University of Nevada Situation," stated, "Professor Richardson has never communicated personally with the Association's Central Office or the Chairman of Committee A." He reaffirmed that the AAUP stood ready to "conduct an investigation in case of an adverse legal decision" and that "a committee of investigation has been constituted, and is ready to act when needed." The chairman of that committee, Robert Brode, in a March 16, 1954, letter, requested that Shannon reexamine the AAUP files in the Richardson case because he had the "impression" that both Richardson and Gray had requested an investigation. He further indicated that the "failure to begin this investigation is entirely a matter of decision in the Central Office."[23]

Shannon, in a somewhat miffed reply to Brode, reaffirmed that there was no letter. He insisted that Brode provide him with the "facts" that created the impression that Richardson had asked for an investigation and support why he thought the source of the delay was to be found in the central office. Brode immediately sent him a photocopy of Richardson's October 21, 1953, letter and suggested that he also recheck the files for a letter from Professor Little also requesting an investigation. Brode further warned that the "Association had been subject to criticism in its failure to act in cases like this." Brode was possibly referring to a May 21, 1953, complaint from Chester F. Cole at Fresno State College who, in reference to the lack of an investigation at UN, stated, "For some years I have thought that the AAUP is too 'talkative' and a little shy on action." In addition to private complaints such as Cole's, there had been write-ups in the press about the AAUP's lack of action.[24]

On March 26, 1954, Shannon received a telephone call from Minard Stout in response to Himstead's telegram advising the president of the creation of an investigative committee and asking his approval of Brode and Wilson as members. Stout informed Shannon that, although he did not know Brode personally, he objected to having anyone from Berkeley on the committee. Stout's objection was based on the fact that Berkeley's AAUP chapter had sent a telegram critical of the Stout administration to a Reno newspaper. He did not mention, however, that Berkeley was Richardson's alma mater. Stout also stated that, although he preferred that there be no investigation at all, if one did take place he would "open the books" and "cooperate fully." The president took this opportunity to inform Shannon that there were "certain 'young Turks' in the Republican Party" (no doubt he was referring to Gary Adams and his supporters) who were trying to "get control of the legislative representation" from Washoe County. This group, Stout believed, planned to take action in the legislature that would be " 'hostile to the University' such as cutting the budget and bringing about a 'rough' investigation of the University." Because he was concerned about the threat that a "badly constituted committee of the Association might be used for political purposes by a small group trying to dominate," he said he would "almost welcome an investigation by a fair minded committee."[25]

Even though requests for an investigation continued to be sent to the AAUP's central office in 1954 and 1955, it was not until May 1955 that an on-site investigation was actually held. Several California chapters of the AAUP had sent observers to the Richardson hearing in 1953, written letters denouncing the university administration's actions, and requested the national organization investigate at that time. Those requests came at a time when the national AAUP, according to Ellen Schrecker, was suffering from inertia. General secretary Ralph Himstead's effort to protect the organization from destruction by the political morass surrounding the Red-scare cases inadvertently created a situation where no decisions at all could be made.[26]

The fact that Himstead initiated an investigative committee in 1953 and later created the final investigative committee in 1955 testifies to his desire to actively protect academic freedom. However, whether it was because he feared that the taint of Communism would damage the association, as Schrecker suggests, or that the sheer volume and complexity of the cases produced by the second Red scare overwhelmed both his ability to delegate tasks and his obsessive attention to minute detail, as Walter Metzger claims, the 1953 investigation did not occur, and the 1955 investigation was held but not published until September 1956 under the leadership of the new general secretary, Ralph Fuchs. It was not until June 1955 that the AAUP finally responded to the *Chicago Tribune*'s charges that "since no allegation of communism was made against Dr. Richardson . . . the AAUP showed only the most perfunctory interest in his case." The *Tribune*'s claim that only Communist cases received attention was inaccurate; close examination of the record would have shown that the national AAUP was not following up on any of its investigations. No Committee A reports at all appeared in the *AAUP Bulletin* between 1949 and 1956, not even for investigations regarding teachers whose problems were not related to Communism.[27]

As more affronts to academic freedom occurred, and after the request by the local chapter for an investigation, the national headquarters of the AAUP set up a new team of investigators who began their query on May 30, 1955. Instead of Professors Brode and Wilson, the team was made up of Charles

Howard, a University of Oregon law professor, and Glenn Bakkum, an Oregon State College sociology professor. They were dispatched to Reno with the mandate from Himstead to "investigate conditions of academic freedom and tenure and faculty-administration relations at the University of Nevada," or, put more bluntly by the *Nevada State Journal,* "to investigate charges that President Minard Stout has attacked academic freedom at the university." The investigation, though mainly concerning itself with the 1953 firing of Richardson, also took testimony on later controversial events and conditions in general. According to local news sources, the investigative team held private hearings between May 31 and June 3, 1955, at which many faculty members, several members of the administration, some of the regents, and even President Stout presented testimony. As a result of these efforts, the AAUP insisted that it had conducted a fair and objective hearing.[28]

Stout in 1972, however, remembered otherwise. The major portion of the investigators' time, according to the former president, was taken up by a limited few who monopolized the agenda and controlled the information the team was given. According to Stout, as the investigation drew to a close with the vast majority of faculty still waiting impatiently to present their side, time was so short that only one spokesman for the entire group could be heard. The implication is that even though Stout and the regents had testified before the committee, the bulk of the information Howard and Bakkum collected was culled from very few sources, most all of whom had a specific agenda: to get Stout.[29]

Bakkum and Howard, on the other hand, maintain that "every witness that the administration at the University of Nevada wanted us to meet and hear" was heard. According to Bakkum, the committee was willing to accept any written deposition that the administration would have cared to submit. In response to Stout's charge that many faculty waited futilely to testify, Bakkum's statement that the committee "continued to hear witnesses from the opposite [AAUP] side until it became clear that the evidence was becoming cumulative and repetitious" implies that only some anti-Stout witnesses were prevented from testifying. Howard and Bakkum emphatically insist, "No one can truthfully say that their side was not heard by us." As far as pro-Stout witnesses were concerned, Howard remembers, "The striking similarity of statements made by persons who testified for the administration in this matter raises some doubt in the minds of the committee as to the probative value of the testimony." He later clarified his meaning: "I did not believe [Stout's] witnesses that such a [dissident] group existed. They told the same story, which sounded rehearsed to me."[30]

From the president's perspective, the AAUP had always been a bane to the educational system and an unnecessary challenge to administrative leadership. His treatment of Richardson and Little as local chapter president and vice president, respectively, was indicative of the antipathy in which he held that organization. That an instigator of the investigation, the local chapter's current president, Lowell Jones, was also from the biology department only confirmed for Stout that he was being singled out for condemnation. Furthermore, the investigative team's independence and its attendant publicity naturally pricked Stout's reactive temperament as they challenged his administrative philosophy. Even though in a taped interview he claimed to always "roll with the punches," during a meeting with students just after the completion of the investigation, Stout's ire at not having had control of the situation was plainly evident. Commenting on the potential results of the AAUP team's survey, he said, "[I]t is only natural for management to be reluctant about the investigation by labor."[31]

Memory being what it is, one may be skeptical of Stout's recollections concerning the conduct of the AAUP investigation. However, that same skepticism must be equally applied to some of his detractors. Russell Kirk's effective but unsupported assertion in his now famous book about Stout's comment to the AAUP around the time of the Richardson hearing is a good example. Stout stated, according to Kirk, that because he was merely trying to get rid of "an obdurate professor who stood in the way of his projected reforms" and had not accused Professor Richardson of Communism, there was no infringement on academic freedom. Many denizens of the conservative world of autocracy overlooked the real meaning of academic freedom, defining it only in relation to Communism. If Kirk is indeed correct in his quotation, then Stout's attitude paralleled that of many mainstream conservatives, including William F. Buckley Jr., who believes that academic freedom leads to atheistic socialism.[32]

In a taped interview, Stout further claims that the final report issued by the AAUP that resulted in censure for the university administration in 1956 was actually the third one written. After the investigative team submitted its report to the central office in Washington, D.C., Stout was sent a copy for his review and response. He later went to Washington and met with the three top officials of the AAUP. In an all-day meeting, Stout pointed out that the report contained sixty to seventy errors of fact, even though the data were there to support the proper conclusions. The chairman finally admitted that the report could not be used. Stout told the AAUP that the university administration would welcome a new team to do a more careful study. But he was informed that there was not enough time to do another investigation. The report was returned to the Oregon professors to be rewritten. The second report was better, but still not correct. It, according to Stout, contained only thirty some errors, which were analyzed in a second meeting with the heads of the AAUP. Again, Stout asked for a new investigative team and even offered to help pay the expenses. But again he was told there was not enough time because the report had to be published. The chairman of the AAUP then sent a man to help the Oregonians rewrite the report once again. The result of this final rewrite was what became the report for censure, and Stout refused to even read it. Despite all the distress, Stout was pragmatic about the report. He told the *U of N Sagebrush,* "I don't believe there is any case where the AAUP has decided in favor of administration."[33]

The records from the AAUP tell a somewhat different account of the creation of the final report that led to censure. The initial report as compiled by Howard and Bakkum ran to more than one hundred pages. Stout was sent a confidential copy of the original report and asked to comment. Whereas he found sixty to seventy errors of fact, the investigative team insisted on the validity of their original findings. Even though the report was supposed to be confidential, somehow a copy of it and a copy of Stout's rebuttal found their way to Denver Dickerson (who, according to Robert Hume, was a close friend of Stout) at the *Nevada State News.* It is interesting to note that Dickerson, in his column "Salmagundi," charged that one of the failures of the AAUP report was "its violation of the basic principles of justice wherein the accused may know who his accusers are, the specific charges against him, and the evidence." This charge sounds very much like the one waged against Stout when he issued the "show cause" letters to the five faculty members.[34]

Dickerson further argued, "The examples of wrongdoing pointed out by this team [Howard and Bakkum] were so absurd, the conclusion so twisted, that a carefully worded rebuttal by Dr. Minard A. Stout [*sic*] caused the hierarchy of the AAUP to submerge the report." It is curious why Dickerson believed that the report was submerged. In fact, the report was not hidden away but was edited at the central office, as is the case with all incoming reports. Therefore, the report was not sent back to the two Oregon professors to be rewritten as Stout claimed, but an edited and shortened version was sent to them for correction and approval. However, as a matter of conjecture, it seems that Professors Howard and Bakkum were not told that President Stout had received a copy of the original. The cover letter sent with the edited draft was dated April 27, 1956, whereas Dickerson's column was dated April 26.[35]

The report was edited and amended three times from the original of more than one hundred pages to the final twenty-seven pages. In addition to Howard, Bakkum, and Stout, the report was edited by Professors Richardson, Little, Gorrell, Hume, Laird, and Harold Brown; former president Malcolm Love; and the members of the AAUP's Committee A on Academic Freedom and Tenure. Responses from Committee A members included: "[T]he revision is a rather anaemic version of the first draft," "I am not always sure of the wisdom of Richardson, but I have no doubt of the folly of Stout," and "This present version seems rather to slur over Stout's really heinous actions." Responses from the five aggrieved faculty varied, but all regretted that the report was not strident enough in its condemnation, that the report did not address the continued attacks on academic freedom after Richardson's dismissal, and that the delay in publication of the report would destroy almost all of its practical value for the UN situation. Professor Brown confined his comments to correcting the misinformation in the report concerning his role in the Richardson case, including that he was "incensed" by Richardson's circulation of the Bestor article.[36]

The only response by President Stout to the final revision was, "It is my understanding that the report has gone to print; and therefore, I will not make any reply to these changes." He thanked general secretary Fuchs for the AAUP's courtesy to his comments on earlier drafts of the report and expressed the hope that Committee A (the censuring body) would "study the total case . . . carefully." The prognosis for escaping censure was not hopeful if the comment by one member of Committee A was any indication. In a note to Fuchs written August 21, 1956, George Stewart commented concerning a proposed follow-up investigation, "I see no need for sending members of committee A to the University of Nevada. As long as Stout remains president, I favor censure."[37]

Finally, the report was published in the autumn 1956 issue of the *AAUP Bulletin,* but, as predicted by many, it seemed to have little impact on the academic world. The censure of the University of Nevada's administration was, according to Robert Gorrell, virtually ignored by the Board of Regents. Most of the members of the board could afford to be indifferent to the AAUP's stand because, in addition to the inherent western independent nature and rejection of outsiders, there was an abundance of teachers looking for jobs. Although fewer applicants sought jobs at UN for a time after the censure decree was issued, according to one faculty member, the situation improved quite quickly after Stout's departure. Stout, on the other hand, firmly asserts that even with the censure "we never had trouble getting faculty or anybody to come with us." Reaction to the censure varied among students, faculty, administration, and the public. Stout believed that "the situation was forced upon us, but the effects are not as serious as some persons would like to have the public think." The local chapter of the AAUP believed that the censure action would be harmful because qualified personnel would be reluctant to join the faculty and students might not want to attend for fear that their diplomas would be worthless. Regent Thompson agreed that hiring would be a problem, but was not surprised at the censure decree, given how the faculty had been treated; regent Hardy did not think the action by the AAUP was serious. The faculty, as with the Richardson case, were split on both sides of the issue, whereas students tended to blame Stout for placing the university in such an adverse position.[38]

Although the AAUP's action may have been an unacknowledged black eye and a small detraction for the administration, it was not without its benefits for the faculty. When Stout and the regents revoked the automatic tenure regulations back in June 1954, it was done on the assumption that new policies for granting tenure would be created before the end of the fall semester. However, by June 1955, those new rules had yet to be formulated. In the intervening year, Stout refused tenure to many professors who would have qualified under the old rules. But, according to Everett Harris, "after the AAUP investigators completed their survey of campus conditions, Stout very suddenly granted tenure to a sizeable number of young professors." Whether as a result of the probe or not, within three months after it ended, Stout proposed and the regents approved tenure or promotion for twenty members of the faculty.[39]

Two very interesting, and somewhat oppositional, events occurred right around this time. As the AAUP was finishing its survey on the Reno campus, it was announced that the editorial staff of the *Artemisia,* the student yearbook, had dedicated the 1955 edition to sociology associate professor Allvar H. Jacobson. The students were going on record as supporting free speech and fortitude. Perhaps their bold but unpopular move was an unintended consequence of the 1954 commencement address given by Malcolm Love, Stout's immediate predecessor as president of UN. In that address, Love urged students to cast out prejudices and intolerances, learn the difference between right and wrong, and study the foundations of the American system. Most pointedly, perhaps, was his statement that "professors who sit in classrooms have one of the greatest responsibilities of our times. They should work not for the reformation of the world, but in search of the truth in their own fields and to insure that the minds of youths are not deceived." It seems the class of 1955 followed his admonition to "Perform your duty. Be good citizens. America can have faith in the future if you honor and defend the ideals for which men have died."[40] Or, perhaps as in Jacobson's case, men who had forfeited their livelihoods.

The second occurrence was a letter sent to the Board of Regents and copied to Jeff Springmeyer, counsel for the legislative commission that was responsible for finding an independent investigative group. The letter, signed by "A.

Taxpayer," was sent from Las Vegas and warned the regents that they had "been sold out by the very group which instigated the investigation, Dissidents on the Faculty." The sellout evidently was the result of the AAUP investigation already conducted on the campus at the behest of the faculty. The writer further warned the regents and the lawmakers that it would be a waste of twenty-five thousand dollars to turn an investigation over to "left-wing Carnegie or other similar Foundations. Or the mostly left-wing College groups." The closing paragraph of the letter revealed the depth of this taxpayer's feelings about western individualism, the pervasiveness of Communism in education, and the need to stand up for Americanism. "It really makes one tremble for the future of America when the LEFTIES can cause a State Legislature to spend $25,000, because its members have been too busy to keep posted on this massive pressure campaign groups like AAUP have come to wage all over the country . . . where any hesitence [*sic*] is shown on the right-wing side."[41]

Although Stout may well have agreed with the above sentiments, and felt sorely tried by the effrontery of the faculty to bring about the "biased" AAUP investigation, he also made an extensive effort to upgrade the salaries and facilities at the institution. However, even those efforts did not go smoothly for him. There were several reasons for the travails Stout faced in his endeavors. Funding and distribution were particularly arduous areas for the president. Naturally, because the legislature was in the midst of trying to create an investigation of the university administration, they were reluctant to appropriate monies for administrative use.[42] In addition, with regent Thompson now on the board, many of Stout's plans did not unanimously sail through to approval, as had been the case in the past.

In the past, Stout could count on the successful passage of his measures because he had always gained each regent's individual support prior to submitting any proposal; however, now Thompson became an unpredictable entity in Stout's calculations. As a result of Thompson's advocacy of the faculty and his public criticism of Stout's administration, there developed a constant undercurrent of tension on the board that had not existed before. More often than not, that tension remained subdued and out of the public arena, but on certain issues, "the electric atmosphere" erupted into the open.[43] A case in point was the president's attempt to get salary increases approved at the June 1955 meeting of the Board of Regents. For the first time in the history of Stout's reign, a regent publicly challenged his choices of salary distribution.

The president had often been accused of manipulating faculty salary increases to favor those who supported him, especially during the Richardson controversy. Walter Van Tilberg Clark, Thomas Little, Arthur Grey, and

Allvar Jacobson had all spoken of his overt salary discrimination in their published resignation letters. Stout, however, maintained that salary increases were submitted to him by the deans and he, himself, never changed any of them. He required the deans to use a twenty-one-point "check sheet" on which to base their evaluations. In addition, regardless of the deans' personal feelings and comments, which were important, each college had a particular amount budgeted and had to spread the money accordingly. Stout's admission that he did, on occasion, ask the deans "why or if they were sure" about a particular increase implies that he had an unspoken power over their decisions, despite his declaration that he "couldn't browbeat his deans."[44]

Now, as Stout presented his list of salary increases to the regents, Thompson challenged his figures and suggested changes. The regent believed that the 1953 legislature had voted an across-the-board 15 percent cost-of-living increase for all faculty. However, many faculty had been discriminated against and did not receive that large of an increase; therefore, he believed that every person who was on the faculty in April 1953 "should be getting paid at least 15 percent more than he was receiving at that time." Thompson further asserted that to not do so would only compound the impropriety committed in 1953. Stout immediately opposed Thompson's idea, not only disagreeing with the across-the-board interpretation, but also stating, "[I]f we do this, we would be saying that we were completely wrong in 1953 and I do not believe we were." At this point in the argument, regent Hardy leaped to Stout's defense and accused Thompson of "attacking the work of the board in 1953 unfairly." He claimed that the board had not been discriminatory in 1953 and was not being discriminatory now, except perhaps in Thompson's avid advocacy of certain faculty.[45] Thompson's motion failed, but wishing to maintain his profaculty position while still preserving his point of disagreement, he abstained from voting on the originally proposed salary-increase schedule. Later in the meeting, however, Thompson made his point more directly when he voted against increasing President Stout's salary for the coming year.

Salary discrimination was not the only point of contention between Thompson and Stout. At that same Board of Regents meeting, a short argument between them ensued over "the manner in which faculty members should be allowed to participate in the operation of university affairs." Stout stated, "An uninformed person should not have the right to place a block in the way of an informed person in another area." He did add, however, that "progress depends on each faculty member having freedom in his own field." Thompson's rebuttal, undoubtedly directed at an earlier statement made by Stout, was that "[t]he great value of a university is that it pools knowledge from many fields." After the regent had expanded on the value and desirability of general faculty meetings, Stout rejoined with, "[I]f you are going to go out of an area to get advice on it, you may as well go down on the street and take a laborer."[46] Thompson, on the other hand, believed that the university had functioned very well while general faculty meetings had been an integral part of its governance.

It was exchanges such as this one between Stout and Thompson that heralded the beginnings of the change in the public's attitude toward Minard Stout and his administration of the university. Even though the majority of members of the Board of Regents were staunchly in his camp, the fact that a regent was speaking publicly and openly challenging Stout's administrative ideology increased public interest. Until this point in time, most of the disapproval had been registered by members of the faculty, whom the average citizen considered spoiled at best and leftist at worst, by elitists who had higher social or political aspirations in mind, and by "outsiders" who would not know what was best for Nevada if someone told them. Current criticism of Stout's administrative techniques was coming from the very source of all his previous support: the Board of Regents. That, coupled with the recent willingness of the notoriously tightfisted legislature to spend twenty-five thousand dollars on an impartial and objective investigation of the entire University of Nevada administrative structure, was causing many in the general public to pay attention to what was occurring up on the hill.

Meanwhile, the legislative commission decided that the proposed investigation should include academic as well as administrative aspects of the university. This change was instituted partly in an attempt to appease lawmakers and others, like "A. Taxpayer," who believed that the "troublemakers" on campus were at least as deserving of investigation as Stout. As a consequence, the counsel began looking for individuals of specific acumen in various academic fields to work with a management-consultant group in an overall team effort. Legislative counsel Springmeyer, in a move reminiscent of the hiring practices of Silas Ross and Minard Stout, said he had asked some of the nation's outstanding educators to recommend individuals for the probe team. Between June and September, however, the thinking of the legislative commission evolved away from a business-oriented management-consultant format and fixed wholly on the idea of an investigative team composed of individuals of various competencies who would survey different aspects of the university community. In order to achieve an effective team, they decided to choose a well-qualified director who would then select the rest of the team members. Although Springmeyer originally recommended acquiring a list of between thirty and forty individuals from which to choose, some historians have suggested that Dean E. McHenry had an inside track for the position of director.

What gives credence to this suggestion is that at the same meeting in which Springmeyer first recommended to the commission that a director be chosen who would in turn select the survey team, McHenry was in attendance.[47] Even with Springmeyer's recommendation, McHenry, a professor of political science at the University of California at Los Angeles, if indeed he had the inside track, was not a shoo-in for the position. The educator, not unknown to Nevada educational circles, brought with him some interesting connections and some troublesome history, along with a penchant for creating more controversy.

During his interview with the legislative commission, McHenry revealed that he "had been offered the post of president of the University of Nevada in 1952 and had refused." This admission brought a quick and pointed reaction from the editor of the *Elko Daily Free Press,* himself a former regent. In an attempt to set the record straight, the editor explained, "To our knowledge Dr. McHenry was never offered the post of president of the university and because of his assertion we feel he is unworthy to be designated as an investigative official. He was one of the last four to be considered when Dr. Malcolm Love was named university president [in 1950]." Silas Ross, in his memoirs, acknowledges that he had met McHenry when he was a candidate for the presidency and that he "thought he was a pretty good fellow, but I thought he was a dean, and everyone else thought he was a dean. But that was his first name." As the prospect of McHenry's being chosen to direct the survey team came closer to reality, the Board of Regents's chairman addressed the issue of McHenry and the UN presidency in a letter to the legislative commission. In response to McHenry's statement, Ross declared, "Dr. Dean McHenry was never offered the position of president of the University of Nevada. . . . He was proposed for the position in 1950, but Dr. Love was selected and appointed. . . . Because of the previous proposal and consideration, he was left on the list of potential candidates in 1952. He was not interested in being a candidate at that time because he was seeking political office."[48] Therefore, the first controversy emanating from McHenry's consideration for the directorship sent mixed signals to the community. He was obviously qualified enough to be considered for the presidency of the university, but at the same time, his less-than-candid description of his interaction with that position created doubts about his capability to be objective during an investigation.

The troublesome history that McHenry brought with him was the same one that haunted many educators of the time: the old bugbear of "Reducation." The legislative commission, impressed by McHenry's comprehensive background as professor, author, legislative adviser, and politician, was brought up short when B. Mahlon Brown of Clark County stated that he had heard that McHenry, during a California political campaign, had been accused of Communistic leanings. McHenry's explanation of the accusation was straightforward and no doubt elicited more than a little sympathy from the lawmakers who understood the risks of political smears during campaigns. The local Reno newspapers carried a full account of McHenry's testimony.[49] It seems that McHenry had from 1943 to 1945 been in charge of an adult education group in Los Angeles known as the People's Educational Center. Over the course of time, the board of directors of the center was infiltrated by Communists and left-wing extremists, and the center ended up on the infamous U.S. attorney general's list of subversive organizations. Prior to that time, however, McHenry had resigned from the board. He had later been given "the fullest clearance" by the ultra-right-wing Tenney committee for whom he was a witness against the center. The smear came when he was running for Congress and his opponent issued a press release alleging that he had been an active adviser of a Young Communist League group. McHenry said he filed a one million–dollar libel suit, but settled out of court for five thousand dollars and an elaborate apology.

Whether McHenry's brush with anti-Communist zealotry caused him any particular difficulty in becoming the director of the survey committee has not been documented. However, the fact that he was considered for the post at all created enough controversy to overshadow anything Joseph McCarthy could have stirred up. Prior to the change of the investigative committee from a management-consultant group to individual members of the academic community, the Board of Regents, President Stout, the Alumni Association, and various student groups had all agreed to support the investigation and to abide by the recommendations of its report. However, after the legislative commission began considering individuals, and especially after it seemed inevitable that McHenry would be chosen as director, the regents and Stout changed their minds.

Board chairman Ross was not mollified by the fact that Springmeyer and his staff had done much research to arrive at a list of thirty people with top reputations in their fields who would be willing to direct or participate in the study. He was even less pleased with the fact that Springmeyer had settled on McHenry as the best choice after "much contact with top educators." Even McHenry's admission that he knew and respected Ross from his earlier dealings with the presidency could not elicit a positive response from the board chairman. Perhaps it was McHenry's promise to see that "evenhanded justice was done" and that he promised to work closely with the legislature during the investigation that caused some to question his objectivity and goals.[50] Both of these promises were anathema to the regents, who already knew what the outcome of the investigation should be.

Whatever the underlying reasons, Ross expressed his complete dissatisfaction with the method of the survey and with its potential director in a sharp letter to each member of the legislative commission. One of his primary grievances was that during the initial legislative discussions about creating an investigative committee, the regents had recommended six organizations from which they had asked the legislators to seek advice on personnel for the probe group. Ross was incensed that the legislative commission had chosen McHenry, who was not on the lists of people proposed by these six organizations, saying, "[H]is name is unknown to the offices of these organizations." Springmeyer explained that he had not heard about Ross's list of organizations because the list had been given to the attorney general. Further, Ross firmly believed that both the board's early support for a thorough study by an impartial group of competent, nationally recognized educators who specialized in land-grant universities and the "verbal assurances" that were made by the legislators had guaranteed the board the right to "concur" in the selection of the inquiry group. His letter continued with the subtle threat that the Board of Regents could no longer honor its agreement to accept the investigation's findings if it did not have confidence in the group.[51] Because the legislators had not kept faith with the board, then the board would not be cooperative either, and the study would, as some legislators feared, be a waste of taxpayer money.

The coup de grace was the lecture Ross gave the legislators on the state constitution: that the university is "to be controlled by a board of regents . . . who are elected by vote of the people of the entire state for four year terms. They are responsible to that electorate." After a week or so of working themselves into a fine lather over Ross's attempt to "cajole, persuade, and intimidate the commission into making a survey team choice favorable to the regents," the legislative commission responded by unanimously selecting McHenry to head the investigation. The regents' response to the commission's obvious fit of pique was silence; they made absolutely no public mention of the commission's action nor further discussed McHenry.[52]

From these inauspicious beginnings, the survey was supposed to produce a balanced, objective, and useful report that would get the University of Nevada back on track and turn it into a viable, progressive institution of higher education of which any state could be proud. But just because the Board of Regents was silent on the issue of the survey team did not mean that the politics of the issue were not being played out in the public arena. The *Reno Evening*

Gazette's editor immediately attacked the legislature for its intemperance and its petulant show of power. The editorial believed the actions of the legislative committee members (but not those of Chairman Ross) would prejudice the survey from the start because in order to be fair and impartial, both sides must have the right to pass judgment on the investigators. He condemned the legislative commission for turning the survey into "an offensive weapon [to be used] by the critics of the university administration."[53]

Not to be left out of the excitement, the university student senate conducted its own inquiry into the selection of McHenry. Associated Students of the University of Nevada (ASUN) president Jerry Mann said that students needed to get beyond all the rumors and find out the facts for themselves. The students were to have met on campus with McHenry on October 13 to obtain his perception of the investigation, but because arrangements for meetings with Stout and Ross could not be made for the same day, the probe leader postponed his meeting with the students. McHenry, however, cognizant of the need for support from as many areas as possible, did meet with the executive committee of the ASUN senate the next day in Carson City and discussed his selection process and his qualifications.[54]

The students also met the following week with legislative counsel Springmeyer, Alumni Association president Samuel B. Francovich, and President Stout to hear both sides of the McHenry argument. Springmeyer reiterated that ninety-two organizations and individuals had been considered for the investigative post. The recommendations of four of the six organizations proposed by the regents had been rejected by the committee because those organizations tended to favor the same "educationist theory" of administration then existing at the university. McHenry had been selected because he favored neither side in the substantivist versus educationist controversy that was plaguing many educational institutions across the country. McHenry, Springmeyer said, came highly recommended and would keep the survey objective. Stout, on the other hand, indicated that neither he nor any of the leading educational organizations he had contacted had ever heard of McHenry. Although admitting that "any good investigation would probably find things wrong in a university," he clarified that only "the recommendations provided by a well-known authority would be good for the university." On a personal note, he added, "If recognized investigators said that I had been wrong, their opinion would carry some weight."[55] Consequently, because McHenry was not nationally "recognized," then neither Stout nor the regents would be bound by the report's recommendations.

President Stout and the Board of Regents were feeling fairly secure in their position as administrators of the university. Most of the dissatisfaction expressed by the students, faculty, and alumni had been kept under control. The regents and the president had gone to great lengths to present a positive image of themselves, to accentuate their successes in growing the university, raising salaries, increasing donations and funding, and meeting the state's educational needs. They believed they had minimized the threat posed by the McHenry investigation and its supporters. Furthermore, they were maintaining control over the ever restless students. Stout's administrative philosophy had taken some punishment, but it appeared to be solid, and the outlook for 1956 seemed bright.

4: Out with Stout

"The University of Nevada has been awarded membership in the National Association of American High Schools. . . . [Academic Vice President William] Wood singled out President Stout for praise. 'We were never even considered for the honor until he became President of this institution.'"[1] So announced a front-page article in the 1957 April Fool's issue of the campus newspaper appropriately renamed for the occasion *U of N Sagemush.* Although the entire newspaper contained spoofs on all types of stories, including the McHenry investigation, this particular article was specifically written with an intended point. With the enactment of the GI Bill after World War II and its renewal after the Korean conflict, the influx of older, more worldly students matured the temperament on campus somewhat. As a result, students resented the patriarchal treatment accorded them by the administration. Instead of being treated as high schoolers, the students desired respect as young adults, demanded to be granted authority over their own behavior, and insisted on being heard. This issue arose several times to challenge the Stout administration, but it became more prevalent as the president attempted to solidify his command.

Two years before this article appeared, President Stout, during an October 1955 talk before the student senate about the pending investigation, made a statement that further irritated students and gave his opponents one more area for which Stout could be attacked. Not only did it reopen the old issues of admission standards and who should be favored with a university education, a sensitive issue with many students, but it also raised the ire of an entire segment of students and many in the community. Stout blithely reported, "Some of the present critics of the administration and the university have been women in Reno, some of whom took classes and got credits without a great deal of difficulty. They prefer the European kind of universities in which college education is limited to a few."[2]

Although his sense of chivalry would not allow him to mention names, it did not keep him from casting aspersions on the character of women students. The actual target of his attack, however, was probably Helen Wittenberg, wife of one of the Richardson attorneys and vocal spokesperson for the Friends of the University. Because his wrath was directed at a woman, he was not at liberty to rely on his old coach's advice to fight fair or foul as the circumstances warranted, so he had to express his frustration tactfully. He had, undoubtedly against his better judgment, attempted to reason with Wittenberg about the Richardson issue. His secretary, Alice Terry, recalls an occasion when he attempted to demonstrate the correctness of his position and to prove that Richardson had, indeed, been insubordinate. After explaining his philosophy and presenting his documentation, however, Wittenberg went away "unconvinced." Stout had made references to Wittenberg at various times since the beginning of her active efforts on the faculty's behalf. It was obvious to some that he was annoyed with her because she was embarrassing the university. According to Robert Gorrell, she was always discovering information and facts that Stout believed need not be divulged.[3] But whatever the purpose of Stout's statement, its innuendo was not lost on his audience. The president's specific and derogatory focus on women did not endear him to a large segment of the public or the student body.

Stout may have been oblivious to the overall nature of his insult, but he did not lose sight of the fact that he needed to try to undercut the McHenry probe. In January 1956, Stout attempted to demonstrate his indispensability by getting the regents' approval to ask Governor Russell to seek a $609,223 emergency appropriation for the university from the special session of the state legislature. The money, according to Stout, was desperately needed for higher salaries, more instructors, and improving the library. He had prepared charts that demonstrated that enrollment had increased twice as fast as had faculty since the fall semester of 1953. Decreasing the teaching load and increasing the salaries were very positive steps toward ensuring a happier, and what he hoped was a more compliant, faculty. But to give credit where it is due, these two steps were also beneficial to the building of a university that would be a viable entity in the mid-twentieth century. Stout and the regents were successful in their efforts, and in February the legislature provided the requested funds for what was termed the biggest growth period of UN's eighty-year history.[4]

In October 1956, after the building program was well under way, Stout had compiled and printed a bulletin titled *Highlights of Progress.* This four-page booklet, prepared by the university's news service under the direction of Robert Laxalt, featured all of the achievements accomplished during Stout's administration. Citizens statewide were informed of the creation of both the College of Education, which would receive accreditation in early 1956 from the American Association of Colleges for Teacher Education, and the College of Business Administration. In addition, the bulletin described the new School of Nursing and the Graduate School, elaborated on the increase in doctorate-level faculty, emphasized the increases in faculty salaries and student enrollment, and described the development and expansion of the Nevada Southern campus. A point of particular pride was the increases in funding from the legislature and the impressive increase in donations and gifts. This presentation was to be followed by two bulletins that would spotlight the changes and improvements Stout's administration had made in the existing colleges and schools, and would highlight the future needs of the university.[5] Bulletins about the achievements of previous administrations were scheduled to be compiled and printed at some later date.

Over the course of the winter of 1955–1956, Dean E. McHenry collected his survey team. Among the members were Arnold E. Joyal, president of Fresno State College; Peter Odegard, former president of Reed College; Richard Lillard, author of books on the West and Nevada; G. Homer Durham, academic vice president of the University of Utah; Robert E. Burns, president of the College of the Pacific; and Carlton C. Rodee, vice chairman of the university senate at the University of Southern California.[6] The credentials of the probe team were very impressive, and, to allay some of the concerns expressed by Stout and the regents, many of the team members had experience with land-grant institutions. However, because each member of the team would be assigned to investigate the area of his expertise, Rodee's portfolio as an expert on faculty issues must have caused some anxiety regarding foregone conclusions.

By early February, plans were under way for the team to begin interviewing faculty members and administrators, with an overall goal of having the survey completed by October 1956. The report would be presented to the legislative commission, which would delay its release until after the 1956 elections; presentation to the entire legislature would not take place until the 1957 regular session. As with seemingly every facet of the UN probe, the delayed release date caused controversy. E. Allan Davis, a former faculty member at Nevada and currently a mathematics professor at the University of Utah, responded with a letter to Governor Russell. In it, he explained that it would be unfair to the voters to deny them the results of the survey before they voted for regents. He believed that because "the top administration of the University (consisting of the Board of Regents and the principle [*sic*] appointee of the Board, the President of the University) is blundering and incompetent," the voters should be allowed to base their votes on the facts that the report would provide.[7]

Students, too, complained that the public needed to know the results of McHenry's investigation in order to make an intelligent choice at the polls. Two separate editorials in the campus paper presented three succinct arguments for early release of the report. Because the regents were elected, the institution was already established in politics; therefore, the report could not make the situation any more political than it was already. It was, according to the *U of N Sagebrush,* unreasonable to expect the voters, who paid for the study, to tolerate four years longer than necessary a situation that they could have changed if they had had the facts. Finally, if the report indicated the need for change, that change had to be made in the Board of Regents because only the board has the ultimate power to correct the situation at the university.[8]

Dean McHenry, not unaware of the raging controversy over the delayed release of the report, took the opportunity in an April meeting with the legislative commission to give a few early recommendations. Whether he did so for the benefit of the voters or the administration is unknown, but his focus had a definite agenda. Some of the areas the investigator listed as needing improvement were faculty morale, the faculty salary scale, retirement benefits, research funds, and office facilities.[9] Stout, who had professed little faith in the results of a study headed by a director who was "not nationally recognized," seemed to have taken heed of McHenry's recommendations. Improvements were made in many of these areas over the next few months.

A second occurrence in early February also created controversy about the probe team. A move was made in the state assembly during the special session of the legislature to add two more members to the McHenry team. Six assemblymen, one from Washoe County, one from Elko County, and four from Clark County (the three largest population centers at the time), introduced a resolution that would add to the committee "an expert on the operation of land-grant colleges and a staff member of the U.S. Office of Education." Members of the legislative commission considered this action not only a "direct slap" at their efforts, but also "an effort to stack the committee in favor of the present university administration, and its president Minard W. Stout." The measure died when it was pointed out that McHenry and the state had already signed a contract and adding new members might abrogate it. As with the controversy over the appointment of McHenry, the regents and Stout stayed out of this new flap, especially since they were not actually implicated in the move. But again, the newspaper editors were more than responsive to this new affront to the UN administration and regents. In his editorial, John Sanford approvingly labeled the six assemblymen as "some of the more conservatives members" and accused Assemblyman Gary Adams, who was the most vocal opponent, of trying to play politics with campus affairs and of trying to ensure that anyone who did not share his views would not be on the committee.[10]

Despite Stout's success at getting more funding from the special session of the legislature and increasing the size and scope of educational facilities throughout the system, tensions were still bubbling under the surface up on the hill. Stout and his lieutenants had all they could do to keep things in check. Student frustrations at being dictated to by what they perceived as an arbitrary surrogate parent had reached a boiling point. According to a front-page article in the January 5, 1956, issue of the *U of N Sagebrush,* shortly before Christmas students had been ready to rampage through the streets with torches aflame and effigies to be strung up. Student complaints reflected their dissatisfaction at not being represented on committees that directly affected their lives. Such important university committees as student affairs, curriculum, orientation, and high school relations all impacted their existence, and they demanded input. But the protest was averted when President Stout, Dean of Student Affairs William Carlson, and Dean of Women Elaine Mobley met with a student committee to "give consideration to all gripes." Stout, claiming that he was unaware that the students were feeling ignored, gave the two deans authority to work with the students and resolve the problems. Despite the president's claim that when he hired someone, he only set the broad fences and then gave him the freedom to operate, he stipulated that the two deans had to clear all of their agreements with him.[11] Whatever agreements were reached between the deans and the students apparently were not entirely acceptable to Stout; by spring, the students could no longer contain their frustration at having their agreements with the deans rescinded.

On March 19, two weeks after McHenry team member Robert Burns, whose portfolio was student services, was on campus examining such matters as administration-student relations, between 150 and 300 students took to the streets of downtown Reno. Even though not a story worthy of front-page coverage, the different perspectives of the event as told by the two local newspapers again showed their respective biases. The headline of the *Reno Evening Gazette,* the paper more strongly supportive of the UN administration and regents, billed the event as a "Two Hour Demonstration Staged by U.N. Students." The banner in the always more critical *Nevada State Journal* shouted, "U of N Students Stage Riot Here." Both reports treated the incident mildly, but the *Journal*'s description implied that the demonstration was organized and included much more detail about the students' antiadministration attitude, whereas the *Gazette* presented it as a spur-of-the-moment occurrence and included the administration's point of view. The students claimed that the demonstration was an outgrowth of the one they had planned the previous December. They declared that because Stout had made certain "concessions" to the student body and later defaulted on them, they had decided to return to their original plan of protest. The students also complained of too many social restrictions and of being treated like adolescents. During the course of the event, the students hung effigies of Stout, Dean Mobley, and Dean Carlson from the Reno Arch, partially burning that of Stout. They shouted "Down with Stout," made comments about Dean Mobley and Silas Ross, and carried banners telling the president to stop running the university like a high school. Nine of the supposedly "more demonstrative" students were "loaded" or "jammed" into a police van and taken to the station. The police took their names and addresses, and then after a lecture, all were released.[12]

It was evidently Dean Mobley who called the police and told them of the "gang" causing a disturbance downtown. Stout said he heard the students pass his office on campus, but thought it was a fraternity run. However, Bob Ferraro, who as a student participated in the event, recalls that before the students left the campus, they marched on Stout's house, chanting, "Down with Stout!" The president came out onto the front porch, looked at the agitated throng, and immediately turned and went back inside without saying a word. Ferraro recalls that Stout's actions indicated that he did not want to discuss the students' concerns that night.[13] This information casts some doubt on Stout's claim of ignorance of the situation or at least the press's statement that Stout, after hearing of the march and warning of possible disciplinary action, conceded that the march was better than "a panty raid." Although Stout's behavior had undoubtedly brought about the students' actions, he need not have felt that he alone among university presidents had been subjected to such student outrage.

UN's history provides examples of similarities between Stout's confrontation with students and those of past presidents. One such is the encounter between President Archer W. Hendrick and students in 1915. In Stout's case, in response to hearing that one of the demonstrators had complained that the administration was treating the students like adolescents, Stout remarked, "Some of them act like that." In 1915, when the student body entered a protest against the administration's decision to change from linen napkins in the dining hall to paper ones, President Hendrick retorted, "[Y]ou shouldn't have *any* napkins, because you don't know how to use them." These students carried posters proclaiming, "We Want Napkins," and also threatened a street demonstration. Also, as with Stout's reign, during the Hendrick presidency, public, faculty, and student complaints led to an investigation of the university by a team from the Federal Bureau of Education. However, whereas that investigation praised the president, it also recommended getting the regents out of politics.[14]

By the following day, President Stout was not quite so affable about the demonstration; perhaps it was only then that he learned the fate of his effigy. What had been "better than a panty raid" now became, "[T]here is no place in a university for mob action [and] students who react in that way do not belong in a university." He made it clear that the fate of the nine detained students was in the hands of the Faculty Committee on Student Affairs, and he would abide by its decision. However, because the committee had not formulated a decision at the time Stout spoke, it would be odd if his statements about mob violence in a university setting did not have a deleterious effect on the committee's deliberations. Once again, the *Gazette*'s editor stepped into the fray. This time, he blasted his rival paper for grossly overstating the incident, gently chided Stout for overreacting, and described the entire incident as merely a case of spring fever that would have been better left ignored. But Stout could not ignore such a challenge to his authority. Upon the recommendation of Dean Carlson and the student activities committee, seven students were expelled. Nine had been taken to the police station, but two had given false names and addresses and were, therefore, untraceable. Stout's formal statement explaining the expulsions reminded students that attending the university was "a privilege provided them through the sacrifices by the people of the state."[15] However, he let Dean Carlson do all of the public speaking on the matter, thus illustrating his contention that his deans were free to act within their own areas.

As further proof of this management technique, Stout encouraged Dean Carlson and Dean Mobley to attend the open meeting called by the student government to protest the expulsions. The meeting ended, however, without the students receiving a satisfactory explanation; Dean Carlson's rationale that the expellees failed to use the proper channels to register their objections and that they were in direct violation of the standards of conduct expected of University of Nevada students was not acceptable to the students. The student government circulated a petition directed to Stout and the Board of Regents that declared, "[W]e feel that the action taken against these students was arbitrary and in violation of the democratic principle of the right of the individual to face his accusers." Even though the expelled students had the right to appeal, the fact that they were "sentenced" before they were allowed to face their accusers smacked of violation of due process; this was somewhat the same scenario that had occurred with the five "dissident" faculty accused in 1953. The *U of N Sagebrush*'s editor proclaimed that expelling students without allowing them their right of due process was setting a dangerous precedent, while Paul Finch, author of the "Out of the Brush" column, labeled Stout and Carlson's expulsion order as deriving from the same irrational emotionalism of which the president had accused the students.[16]

Of the seven students who were expelled, one retained a former Richardson attorney and member of the Friends of the University, Bert Goldwater, to appeal his case. Attorney and Alumni Association member Sam Francovich represented five others, and the seventh, it was discovered, was no longer a student. Before any court action could commence, however, Reno police chief T. R. Berrum wrote a letter to Stout in which he vouched for the cooperativeness of the students who had been picked up and also emphasized that most of the detained students were chosen at random as an incentive for the crowd to disperse. He urged Stout to reconsider the expulsion order. Stout, however, would not make that decision. A copy of the chief's letter was also sent to each member of the Faculty Committee on Student Affairs, but they could not, for whatever reason, reach a decision either. On March 27, a conference was held among the committee, Stout, and Attorney General Harvey Dickerson. Dickerson, agreeing with the student government's earlier concerns about the denial of due process, strongly recommended rescinding the expulsion order. Stout left the meeting saying that the committee had to decide and he would abide by its decision.[17] The expulsions were rescinded and the students reinstated; Stout accepted the decision.

To add fuel to the flames of controversy on the hill, Stout took a public opportunity to demonstrate his authority and to prove, incidentally, that the students had a right to feel as though they were being treated as high schoolers. On the Friday after the expelled students were reinstated, President Stout, ASUN president Jerry Mann, and Alumni Association president Bill Parish were the guests on a local television panel show. Ostensibly, the topic for discussion was student-administration relations on a national scale, with the agreement that the recent local problems at UN would not be discussed. According to Mann, however, after he and Parish each spoke for the allotted five minutes on the prescribed topic, Stout not only "kept his comments on local issues" but also monopolized the rest of the time by speaking for twenty-one minutes. He humiliated the ASUN president when he compared the recent student demonstrations and the resultant administrative actions to a parent punishing misbehaving children.[18] As the embodiment of the university, Stout no doubt believed he had the right and the duty to clarify to the public this issue that had recently caused him so much embarrassment. The host of the show, Denver Dickerson, failed to impose the rules on Stout's speech, but promised to try to arrange another show at which the students could present a rebuttal to the president's comments.

Even though the student reinstatement may have cost Stout a round in the battle for vindication of his administration, he was still attempting to win the overall victory. In late April, it was announced that the faculty had received a "record pay boost." Stout had secured regent approval to grant pay hikes that guaranteed each member of the faculty at least a 15 percent increase, some more than 30 percent, with an average of about 25 percent. Harkening back to the argument between regent Bruce Thompson and President Stout over the 1955–1956 pay increases, it seems as though the president was subtly agreeing with the regent that he and the board had indeed been completely wrong in the 1953 salary awards. But upon examination of the salary schedule for 1956–1957, as published in the Board of Regents's meeting minutes, it is obvious that if Stout saw the light, he did so only dimly. Discrimination in salary awards was still a prominent feature of the 1956–1957 distribution, and the earlier inequities were, as Thompson feared, only perpetuated. For instance, Ira LaRivers, who had testified for the administration in 1953, was awarded a 32 percent increase, whereas Frank Richardson received 17 percent. Raises for other major participants in the Richardson controversy varied; "dissidents" Charlton Laird, Robert Hume, and Robert Gorrell each received 18 percent increases; administration supporter Alfred Higginbotham received 21 percent; and Richardson defender Harold Brown, who had earlier taken a pay cut, received 31 percent, but was moved to a twelve-month contract.[19]

Although any pay hike is a welcome increase, for at least one faculty member, who quite naturally wished to remain anonymous, the anxiety within the university community and the degradation of the campus's reputation were not worth any amount of money. He is quoted as saying, "I would be glad to return the money if only the administration would be changed." Stout interpreted complaints about salary as merely representative of the usual faculty ingratitude. He said that in the case of one faculty member who received the "biggest raise he ever got but heard someone else got a few hundred dollars more[,] he blasted me in the paper."[20] These inequities among the faculty salaries, along with the many other complaints against the Stout administration, all became issues in the upcoming 1956 election campaigns for the Board of Regents.

Chairman Silas Ross let it be known in late April that he would retire at the expiration of his 1956 term. He had begun serving on the board in 1932 and had continually held the chairmanship from 1937; he had spent twenty-five years serving the people's interest. After a quarter century of dedicated service, during which he had, in regent Roy Hardy's early words, "served most honorably and nobly," the end of 1956 was a quintessential milestone from which to step down. But perhaps, too, Ross was tired of the disquietude on campus, the flak from the community that was descending upon the board, and the rancorous division among the regents themselves. The nature of President Stout's administration seemed to some to become more obvious and entrenched as his tenure lengthened. If, as Stout claims, Ross had given him the authority to be his own man and had promised to leave him alone to do his job, the chairman, by 1956, may well have believed the situation at UN was beyond his control.[21] Also, the ultimate action of firing Stout, though always a possibility, would reflect very badly upon Ross's reputation. He had consistently and vigorously supported the president's actions for so long that to admit that he had been wrong would be personally devastating. By retiring, therefore, the public focused on his long, selfless career as a standard-bearer of the university; any dishonor that followed the release of the McHenry study, then, would be aimed at "the regents," not at Ross personally.

Two open seats on the board plus the politicized nature of the situation created a natural attraction for candidates in the 1956 election. In addition to Ross's retirement, Archie Grant's term was expiring. Grant, however, was running for reelection. New contenders included local physician and alumni member Fred Anderson, Las Vegas hotel owner William Elwell, Reno attorney Albert Hilliard, and Elko County district attorney Grant Sawyer.[22] Anderson, who filed in April before Ross had announced his retirement and had criticized the situation at UN, was a local favorite. Proof that conservatism, however, still had a strong foothold in Nevada was seen in the results of the primary election. The voters, by their wide margin for Anderson, showed that they believed a change in the governing structure at the university was necessary. But by the same token, that Grant came in second in the balloting indicated that the people did not want radical change. The voters' complete rejection of Hilliard, who had been a regent before and was the candidate with the most radical proposals for changes in the university administration, demonstrated that excessive reaction was detrimental to conservative progress.

By October 1956, cracks were beginning to appear in the public support for Minard Stout. The *Reno Evening Gazette,* long a staunch supporter of the Board of Regents, and Chairman Ross in particular, had always tried to put a positive spin on the Stout administration. However, during the campaign for regents, the attitude of the newspaper showed a subtle shift by its presentation of the candidates just weeks before the general election. The *Gazette*'s "Know Your Candidates" article provides another excellent example of how news headlines and information placement are intentionally directed toward influencing public opinion. The first half of the article was dedicated to the local favorite, Dr. Fred Anderson. It described his native Nevadan background and his devotion to public service. There followed a pointed but subtle paragraph that carried the message that a change on the board was of vital interest to the public: "It has become fairly apparent that sweeping changes are likely at the university should Anderson and Elwell or Sawyer win the two vacant seats. Changes undoubtedly will come slower with the reelection of Grant."[23]

Continuing the placement strategy, the latter half of the article presented the policy statements of Elwell and Sawyer, with a final small paragraph describing Grant's history, including the fact that he had run unsuccessfully for other state posts.

The legislative commission, too, attempted to influence the election of the Board of Regents. It released the McHenry investigation report on October 25, sixteen days before the election on November 9. Delaying the release of the report had been a point of contention for many months, even though all parties, including legislative counsel Jeff Springmeyer, had agreed to the delay until after the election. Whatever the reason for the early release, public demand or politics, it demonstrated just one more way in which power was slipping away from Silas Ross and the board. But the regents as a whole, as was becoming their habit when the tide flowed against them, were restrained in their discussions about the early release. Both Ross and Stout made the point that because the report had been labeled as preliminary, it should not have been released until it was finalized by the McHenry group. Stout, whose leadership style was a focal point of the report's criticism, also alluded to the "excellent political technique" in the timing of its release. Even though the regents were miffed that excerpts of the report were published in the newspapers before copies were given to the board, Bruce Thompson reminded the board that cooperation from the legislature on funding issues would result only if the regents paid some attention to the McHenry team's suggestions.[24] Ross, on the other hand, wanted to make no commitment until there was a final report available.

The report, *The University of Nevada: An Appraisal—the Report of the University Survey,* dubbed the *McHenry Report,* presented a fairly comprehensive study of all aspects of the university. But statements in the report, such as "the students were almost evangelistic in their zeal against the administration," caused some to question the depth of its objectivity. The two Reno newspapers and the *U of N Sagebrush* all ran extensive excerpts from the report during the last week of October and the first two weeks of November. Several of the investigation's primary findings were specifically highlighted by the media and undoubtedly directly affected the upcoming election. One important recommendation was the need to "overhaul" the Board of Regents.[25] Although the report did not advocate removing any current members, or not reelecting them, it did recommend increasing the board to nine members and also making membership appointive instead of elective. In addition, the report extended a judiciously worded but equivocal compliment to Silas Ross as retiring board chairman.

> His decision not to run for re-election in 1956 and his subsequent retirement bring to an end an era of University history. . . . In the wake of Mr. Ross's retirement, many changes will be in order. The Board, so long led by one man who knew the University intimately, will no longer be closely held. Board members of the future surely will be unable to equal the time and attention he gave to campus affairs. The timing is right for a larger and more representative Board.[26]

The *McHenry Report* was devastating to Minard Stout. A point of vital importance that the *New York Times* brought to the public's attention was that the report "said the dissension was largely the result of 'quasi-military' rule by Dr. Stout." Stout's philosophy, then, was to blame for the report's finding that "Academic Freedom was threatened because faculty members feared retaliation in salary and promotion opportunities." In accordance with Stout's military training and his own sense of hierarchical order, the power to control wages and jobs belonged in the presidential purview. The report further targeted a topic that was part of the original contention between faculty and administration, one that specifically struck at Stout's expertise. It indicated that "the university appeared to be moving in the direction of a trade school." It said the administration had shown "a bias in favor of vocational education as against education in the basic disciplines of liberal arts and sciences." In that vein, the report criticized the administration's arbitrary creation of a College of Business Administration without the benefit of general faculty and legislative consultation, and for developing the College of Education so quickly and so extensively that its educational structure and programs suffered. On the subject of admissions, the original source of agitation in 1953, the report echoed Frank Richardson's concerns that allowing unqualified and unmotivated students to attempt college-level work often results in failure that causes unnecessary frustration for the student.[27]

The report, in following its legislative mandate, made a thorough study of the university administration, in particular, Minard W. Stout. The report attempted to be a balanced presentation of all sides of the controversy. For instance, it listed nine of Stout's achievements that had a "tonic effect" on the university. It also listed nine "indictments" against him. The nine achievements consisted of twelve lines of text, while the nine detriments required one and one-half pages. In addition, there were another two pages of indictments against the administration in general, including the acquisition of the presidential "mansion"; Stout's appointment as professor of education with tenure; his bestowing professorships and salary increases on the deans he brought in from the "outside," even those who had never taught, especially "at a time when he was under fire or severe criticism"; and the excessive granting of travel requests to Stout and the other administrative officers.[28]

The report's ten-page chapter on recommendations contained thirty-six recommendations, three changes to the state constitution, and twenty "major statutory changes." The number-one recommendation was the "restoration of faculty participation" in governance. The team surveyed each of the individual colleges, with the exception of Arts and Science. Some in the community believed that this omission represented a bias because most of the complaints against Stout came from that college. A local well-respected historian, Effie Mona Mack, issued a digest made up of the opinions of "many persons" who had read the *McHenry Report.* Her preface summarized the overall opinions, including concerns that the report was sloppily done, its polling was too informal to be accurate, and it was superficial. She summed up her findings, and presumably those of her participants, by saying, "[I]t seems to be, in many respects, a criticism of the present administration rather than an appraisal of the University of Nevada."[29]

The *McHenry Report*'s revelations, already known to most Nevadans, suddenly became more important because complaints that had been previously bantered about in newspapers were now being confirmed by an "official" source. Consequently, the races for the regents' seats became more intense. Each of the new aspirants tried to outdo the others by claiming fealty to the recommendations of the *McHenry Report* and declaring his intentions to solve the problems on the hill. The incumbent, Grant, said as little as possible about the report, and continually supported the past actions of the regents. In the end, Nevadans decided once again that they wanted change but only on a limited scale; they elected Dr. Fred Anderson and reelected Archie Grant. Once the board was seated, however, Grant, the new chairman, no longer hesitated to make known his feelings about the early release of the report. He stated that the report was released in a move to defeat him at the polls; it was a political maneuver to discredit him, Minard Stout, and the administration.[30]

The reconstitution of the board in January 1957 provided regent Bruce Thompson with a fellow anti-Stout compatriot in Fred Anderson. Hence, the board began functioning on a three-to-two basis whenever there was a contentious issue involving the president. But by still being able to count on three supporting votes, Stout was able to carry on business as usual, despite the *McHenry Report.* The only real differences he faced were that his recommendations were now being challenged by two regents. Public awareness of those challenges grew proportionally. In addition, the legislature was back in session and could begin to take actions based on the report's recommendations. Even though the Board of Regents was a separate entity created by the constitution and could not be policed by the legislature, the lawmakers knew they had the power of the purse through which to exert pressure.

That Stout was still in a position to wield considerable power was made manifest in January when he went before the regents to challenge the *McHenry Report.* Taking a lesson from the structure of the Jacobson hearing, Stout prevailed upon his deans and other administrators to testify about inaccuracies in the study. The criticisms ranged from a very detailed presentation by Garold Holstine of the College of Education, a Stout appointee and second highest-paid dean, to the less involved testimony from Vernon Scheid of the School of Mines, who had been hired by Malcolm Love. Holstine, whose college received much criticism, presented an extensive list of what he said were errors in enrollment figures, number of courses that were taught, and other statistical data; Scheid, who agreed with the recommendations for his school, commented that he and some of his faculty had "little faith in the general report." It is interesting to note that after Stout's deans and administrators spent most of the day presenting their criticisms, the president then presented a "series of recommendations consolidating faculty views on the entire document." The accuracy of the "faculty views" presented by Stout, given his handling of earlier faculty vote counts and such, was certainly open to question. Again, the bias of the administration-oriented *Reno Evening Gazette* was obvious in its handling of the meeting. The front-page headline shouted, "Deans Criticize U.N. Report"; the story presented much of the testimony of the deans, but totally ignored faculty comments.[31]

The two issues emanating from the *McHenry Report* that became major foci of all factions involved were increasing the board membership and faculty participation in governance. On the first issue, action had to wait until legislation was introduced to increase the board's membership. Protagonists and antagonists, then, could only register their opinions on the makeup of the board in the hope of speeding up or delaying the legislature's action. Consequently, the point of active focus became the faculty and its rightful position in the governing structure of the university. Even though Stout sought to maintain his position as spokesman for the faculty, the old bane of the faculty circumventing the administration to go to a higher authority was still a factor in the functioning of the hill. In the event that the faculty views, as presented by Minard Stout, were not as accurate as possible, some faculty were giving their assessments directly to regents Thompson and Anderson.

At the February 28, 1957, Board of Regents meeting, a debate ensued between Anderson's proposal for faculty governance and one presented by President Stout. Anderson recommended that the faculty be made a part of the administration by giving them advisory "legislative jurisdiction" in certain areas with board approval, and also setting up a faculty senate with representation reflecting the size of the colleges and with an elected chairman. Stout's tentative plan also mentioned a faculty senate that he described as made up of one representative from each college and chaired by the academic vice president. The faculty, according to Stout, were members of the professional staff who were delegated the responsibilities of instruction, research, and service, and were also responsible for improving instruction, courses of study, research, academic standards, and faculty-student relations. The faculty might, according to Stout's plan, study educational policy and make recommendations to the Academic Committee, but the academic vice president was to be a member of each committee and a copy of the minutes was to be filed with the president immediately following each meeting.[32]

All in all, the Stout plan did not provide for the free flow of ideas, especially with the president's handpicked lieutenant as chair and the immediate filing of meeting minutes. A ten-member committee, which Stout assured regents was the result of democratic action, had already been appointed to study the question of faculty organization. Anderson, however, informed the board and the president that many faculty members had told him they believed that the committee had not been a democratic creation, but rather had been "shoved down their throat."[33] The general outcome of the meeting was a three-to-two vote not to send any recommendations to the faculty on how to organize but to accept whatever the faculty recommended. The rationale behind these moves was simple. Archie Grant, Roy Hardy, Louis Lombardi, and President Stout rejected sending any recommendations, they said, because they were concerned that the faculty might interpret them as a "stamp of authority." Their willingness, however, to accept whatever organizational plans the faculty committee developed was a safe move because of Stout's acumen for "democratically" selecting committee members.

The need for a faculty senate had been strongly recommended by the *McHenry Report* as well as by the local chapter of the AAUP, whose plan was submitted to the administration and the Board of Regents and may have figured prominently in both Anderson's and Stout's proposals, albeit from different interpretations. It is interesting to note that Anderson's proposal was an almost verbatim rendition of that proposed by Professor Gorrell in the Faculty Forum meeting of February 21. Gorrell's proposal was voted down in the forum because it was believed that there were no specific rules governing the faculty and that the faculty had no power to act on its decisions. A plan more in the manner of Stout's proposal was made by Professor Thomas T. Tucker, chairman of the Department of School Administration and Supervision and director of school surveys. He recommended that a committee made up of one representative from each college be formed to study the proposal to establish a faculty senate and to report their findings to the Faculty Forum at a later date. In a comment obviously directed at Stout, strangely absent from the Faculty Forum minutes but reported in the *U of N Sagebrush,* agriculture professor James Kidwell pointed out that "prior to September 1, 1952, the University had one kind of [faculty] organization and since then another."[34]

On March 2, 1957, the state legislature began working its way toward increasing the Board of Regents from five members to nine. Assemblymen Archie Pozzi, Robert Vaughan, and Bruce Barnum introduced AB 342 with the intention of examining and regulating "the number, election, term, compensation, expenses and reports of the Board of Regents; the appointment, qualifications and duties of the President of the University of Nevada; [and] qualifications and salaries of the academic staff," among other things. Also introduced in the assembly was AB 469 that intended to create "a new provision relating to academic self government by creating a Faculty Senate and delegating certain powers thereto." This bill, according to the *Reno Evening Gazette,* would require that the faculty be consulted by the regents on the appointment of a new president. Both of these actions had been recommended earlier by the legislative commission soon after it adopted the *McHenry Report,* and both had incurred a reaction from the regents. Grant and Hardy, though agreeing that faculty participation in university affairs was desirable, believed that it was an internal affair and should be handled without interference from the legislature. Stout, however, was concerned that if the faculty were given consultative authority with the board, the "president will become nothing but an errand boy between the faculty and the regents." Neither the regents nor the president need have worried about AB 469 making faculty participation mandatory; the bill was referred to the assembly Committee on Education and was never heard of again. Grant, who said he "saw nothing wrong with enlarging the board to seven or nine members," did not actively campaign for the change.[35] Stout was especially skeptical of the recommendation for enlarging the board and warned that appointing its members would not eliminate its political nature. The fact that in the 1950s the vast majority of boards of regents nationwide were appointed and that the average number of members was nine did not deter the administration from attempting to make these changes seem like a personal attack on it and the three original regents.[36] Stout charged that these changes would make the regents responsible to the legislature, or "to [legislative counsel] Springmeyer for the 22 months of the biennium when the legislature is not ordinarily in session." He then concluded with a subtle threat that if this situation did indeed occur, he might leave, as he had taken the job at Nevada because of the "arrangement between the board and its powers and the president and his powers."[37]

In addition to the protests of Stout, the majority of the regents, and other conservatives in the state, Senator Newton Crumley also had reservations about AB 342. Although he agreed that the board should be increased to nine members, he rejected the idea that the situation at UN was an emergency. Both the assembly and the senate had declared the emergency status of the situation for two reasons: one was that because it was late in the session, such a status would dispense with the second reading and therefore expedite the process of passing the bill, and the second was that immediately upon the signature of Governor Russell, the legislature would begin appointing the four temporary board members. Crumley stated he would vote against the bill because "[i]n view of the dubious nature of the basis on which Assembly Bill No. 342 authorizes this Legislature to elect four Regents, I consider the bill to be extremely poor legislation. In my opinion, the declaration of an emergency at the University of Nevada constitutes a subterfuge to circumvent our Constitution." Senator Charles Gallagher's succinct response codified Crumley's concerns. "Unless the bill reaches the Governor early for signature, there will not be time for the Legislature to make its appointments before tomorrow night [March 21, the end of the 1957 session] and in this case, the bill might just as well not be passed." As a result, AB 342 passed the senate on a vote of fourteen to two, was reported back to the assembly, and was sent to the governor the same day. Just as Senator Gallagher predicted, a mere hour after Governor Russell signed the bill, a joint session of the legislature met and appointed Caliente rancher and former Speaker of the assembly Cyril Bastian, Ely druggist N. E. Broadbent, Grant Sawyer, and William Elwell, the latter two of whom had run in the 1956 election, to fill the four vacancies.[38]

However, Attorney General Harvey Dickerson, echoing a charge by Senator Crumley, challenged the appointments as being unconstitutional because "it took from the duly qualified electors of the state the right to elect members of the board of regents by popular vote." Dickerson did not mount this challenge because of any special predilection toward the Board of Regents or the administration, but because he was concerned that without the state supreme court's passing judgment on the constitutionality of the appointments, "there may be a question as to the legality of the contracts and other matters handled by the nine-man board." Because board chairman Grant had charged that "the plan to enlarge the board was a maneuver to fire President Minard W. Stout," perhaps the attorney general did not want to run the risk of the termination being overturned.[39] The supreme court agreed with Dickerson that although the legislature could increase the size of the board, it could not appoint the members, and the four were duly removed, whereupon Governor Russell immediately reappointed the same four to hold the seats until the next general election, which would be held in 1958. From this point forward, Stout's actions faced a six-to-three challenge.

In the meantime, other events were occurring, one of which was the honoring of Silas Ross for his long years of service. The first step was to construct Silas Earl Ross Hall, which was the first state-financed construction project in more than a decade. It provided new, much needed space for classrooms and offices that had been housed in unsightly World War II Quonset huts for so many years. The dedication of Ross Hall took place on April 14, 1957, but it was not without its irony. The formal resolution signed by the Board of Regents and placed in the cornerstone of the building contained the following statement: "[I]f the University of Nevada is the lengthened shadow of a man, that man is Silas E. Ross." These words, taken from Ralph Waldo Emerson's essay "Self-Reliance," also appeared earlier in the *McHenry Report:* "If the University of Nevada is, since the retirement of President Walter E. Clark the 'lengthened shadow of a man,' that man is Silas E. Ross."[40]

The effects of the *McHenry Report* recommendations and of the increased board made themselves felt in many small but important ways. At the May board meeting, it was agreed that, given the difficulty in "obtaining money for salary increases, the President's salary would not be increased at this time, [already the highest in the state at seventeen thousand dollars] and that the perquisites to the office [would] remain the same." Another example of how the board was beginning to take back its power from the president can be seen in the case of associate professor William C. Miller. In June 1957, Miller had petitioned the board to grant him a promotion to full professor. He felt justified in doing so because his department head had recommended the advancement and because he held a Ph.D. and had taught for twenty-four years with no promotion for the past ten. But Miller had not followed administrative channels in his effort to gain the promotion, having gone directly to Academic Vice President William Wood instead of through the Academic Committee. Even though Grant Sawyer moved that Miller be given the promotion, the petition was rejected. But the regents did adopt a motion requiring that in "all recommendations for change in personnel—salaries, tenure or promotion, a formal vote be taken, a record kept of each vote and the voting record be submitted to the Board of Regents, together with a record of all formal actions taken." No longer, then, would the board merely accept the president's word, and no longer could he manipulate committee votes without the committee members being held liable for explanations. In August, Miller again petitioned for promotion to the rank of professor, this time through the proper channels. According to Stout's testimony before the regents, Miller's department had approved the promotion nine to five. The request was then reviewed by the Academic Committee who voted zero to seven against. The result, Stout said, was a nine-to-twelve vote against, and therefore he was not recommending the promotion. Sawyer, after reviewing the situation, moved that Miller be promoted to professor and given a two hundred–dollar raise.[41] The vote on the motion was the six anti-Stout members voting aye and two pro-Stout members voting nay, with only Lombardi abstaining. It was fast becoming obvious to Stout that he was not going to be able to influence the board to the same extent he had in the past. In addition, he was now being held accountable for the actions of his administrators, so if he directed their actions, he could no longer pass the buck back to them. The six regents did not always vote against Stout's proposals, but when those proposals seemed arbitrary or vindictive or merely intended to demonstrate his authority, the six opposition votes were fairly consistent.

By September, the regents had set up a five-man committee to meet regularly throughout the school year with faculty and students. This move was a tremendous blow to Stout's authority because it paved the way for students and faculty to go around the president and seek satisfaction directly from his bosses. Chairman Grant, who was probably not wholly in favor of the committee given his attitude about bosses and workers, appointed his two fellow pro-Stout regents to the committee in addition to Sawyer, Bastian, and Thompson. The committee was designed to hear student and faculty recommendations regarding university policy and affairs, which in turn would be submitted directly to the full board, evidently sidestepping the administration completely. This Grievance Committee soon proved its effectiveness when history and political science professor Austin E. Hutcheson went before it after he had been recommended for promotion by his department head and his dean but was turned down by the administration. Hutcheson was awarded the promotion and a salary increase.[42]

Evidently, the breaking point between the board and Stout came during the October 4 board meeting when President Stout and Vice President Wood recommended increasing the administrative overhead by promoting Marilyn Horn to the position of associate director of home economics with a two thousand–dollar raise. Regents Thompson and Anderson challenged the recommendation because they believed that the university's administrative overhead was already too high. Furthermore, the director of the home economics school had no more administrative problems than anyone else and therefore did not need an assistant. They also expressed concern that the home economics school would develop the same problems for which the College of Education had been criticized in the *McHenry Report,* one-man departments. Stout, Wood, and Grant all supported the recommendation, and Bastian indicated he would go along if it were really necessary. Stout, refuting the McHenry findings, maintained that the administrative expenses at UN were not as high as in most other universities. Horn's promotion and raise were finally approved. But the rancor among board members made it obvious that, under the current conditions, the contention on the board was only going to worsen. This challenge, only the latest of many, no doubt made it obvious to the president that the autonomy he had held under the Ross board was not recoverable; his verbal agreement with the board as to his authority had been breached. With the assured support of only three of the nine board members, Grant, Hardy, and Lombardi, his control of governance at UN was severely and permanently weakened. The next day, October 5, 1957, bowing to the inevitable, Stout submitted his resignation. The only public comment he made was his resignation statement to the board: "Gentlemen, I wish to request that I be relieved of the duties of the President of the University of Nevada as of July 1, 1958."[43] He did not, however, relinquish his tenure.

As word of the resignation spread, the two camps polarized. The regents naturally followed their usual three-to-six split, whereas the faculty, administrators, legislators, and general public chose sides according to their own prejudices. It was generally agreed by all sides that the increase in the number of regents had been the instrumental final impetus of the "get Stout" faction. The appointed regents, however, all denied being specifically instructed to remove the president. Later, when it became obvious that Stout was asked to resign, Fred Anderson said that the move had been made so the president could "save face" and not encounter the stigma of being fired.[44]

The acrimonious board meeting of November 2 brought to light the "behind the scenes" actions of the six anti-Stout members who had met and decided Stout had to go. Later, to add legitimacy, Grant and Lombardi were brought into the group. Hardy, livid at the action of the "rump" meeting, was even more so by having "gotten the deep freeze treatment." He was further embarrassed by not having learned of the requested resignation until he was called by the newspapers. Hardy's complaint that the new regents had been handpicked with an agenda to solve the Stout problem did not seem to trigger a reminder that he and the other regents had handpicked Stout to solve some problems for them. Bastian, however, was prescient enough to remark that the regents, perhaps more than Stout, were to blame for the problems at UN because they had not set policies that would have limited the president's monopolization of power.[45] With no surprise to anyone, the vote to accept

Stout's resignation was six to two with a letter from Lombardi supporting Hardy and Grant.

At the same meeting, Thompson added a little more friction to the situation by proposing a "presidential selection advisory committee" composed of four regents, two administrators, three faculty members, the president of the alumni association, and the student body president. This proposal, in essence, was another slap at the autocratic techniques of the current administration that were always supported by Grant and Hardy. Hardy, still smarting from his earlier confrontation with his fellow board members, disapproved of seeking faculty advice, saying, "It may be democratic, but it's damn poor business," and adding that no mining company asked its foreman who should be a new manager. Eventually, the decision to have a faculty committee involved in presidential searches was adopted. The final version of the committee was made up of one representative from each college except the College of Nursing, one representative of the Nevada Southern branch, and one representative of the university services groups, with three other faculty members to be elected at large.[46] This committee was instrumental in hiring Stout's replacement.

Roy Hardy was able to get a little revenge when he informed the board that the firing of Stout had cost the university a one million–dollar gift. He may have been referring to the bequest of one and one-half million dollars that Noble Getchell had put in his will for the university. According to Stout, he had cultivated Getchell as a friend, and consequently the banker and mining tycoon had stood by him through all his adversity. As a consequence of their friendship, he had bequeathed the money to the university. But when the regents asked for Stout's resignation, Getchell changed his will. Stout relates that in a later encounter with Getchell, the tycoon chuckled over the fact that the Board of Regents had tried to win back his support by "[n]aming the library for me. Damn fools, they're not going to get that money!" There may be some truth in Stout's recollection, at least as far as Getchell's eccentricities were concerned. Silas Ross remembers that Getchell was a person who did not suffer affronts graciously. Getchell, according to Ross, had made a practice of giving scholarships to the top graduates of Lander County's two high schools, but he stopped the awards because he never got a "thank-you" from the students.[47]

At the October 24, 1957, meeting of the Faculty Forum, Stout clarified his resignation and put the faculty on notice that they had not "gotten" him. The president explained that on October 6, regents Grant, Lombardi, and Thompson had come to his office and explained that in a meeting the night before, the rest of the regents had decided to ask for his resignation. He reminded them that "when I took the assignment I told the Board of Regents when they lost confidence in me they could have my resignation simply by asking for it." After a few remarks about all the improvements he had made in the institution, he left the faculty with the proclamation that "there is no disgrace in being fired from a job under certain circumstances." In yet another irony, Stout, when faced with dismissal, responded in exactly the same manner he had taken exception to in Frank Richardson. According to his secretary, Alice Terry, "[H]is thinking was that he had done what he believed was right, and he should see it through. He still didn't think that he had done the wrong thing."[48]

In early November, Stout, while on a trip to Chicago, gave an interview to a reporter from the *Minneapolis Tribune.* In it, he blasted the Board of Regents for being "packed" by a legislature that had a surplus of lawyers who were bored with divorce cases. He further claimed that Frank Richardson, who had spent more time going around the campus trying to stir up trouble than anything else, was merely the front man for a small faculty "central committee" who wanted to run everything. The AAUP censure did not mean anything because the report was largely written before the committee conducted its on-the-scene investigation. In summary, he told the reporter that since his resignation, people from all over came to realize what a great job he had done and were calling him a hero.[49] Needless to say, Stout's comments raised the ire of many in Nevada, not the least of whom were members of the Board of Regents. However, because most of the regents wanted to get the trauma of the past five years behind them and start building a future for the state's only university, they remained mute on the Stout interview. Even though no public discussion of the interview ever took place, Stout had undercut much of the support he had accumulated. He was definitely no longer a "hero" to many in the Silver State.

Minard W. Stout's public denigration of Nevada, questions about unallocated faculty salary funds, and his reluctance to grant pay increases to part-time athletic coaches all militated against his remaining at the helm of the university any longer than was necessary. Consequently, the regents met with him in special session on December 18, 1957, and in twenty minutes, probably their shortest meeting on record, reached an agreement with Stout to terminate his contract as of December 31. They further agreed to pay him $12,500 for the time remaining on his contract and let him live in the presidential house until April 1, 1958, in return for his agreement to surrender his academic tenure. An editorial in the *Nevada State Journal* found it "heartening that for the first time in several years, all members of the University of Nevada board of regents and the president of the university were in accord in a major matter affecting the president."[50] Academic Vice President William R. Wood was named acting president until the position was officially filled.

Stout's departure merely completed the natural administrative cycles in higher education. According to Paul Westmeyer, professor of higher education at the University of Texas at San Antonio:

> Unless the person is ineffective and retiring, a university president shapes the university to his/her own pattern. Regardless of the philosophy of the institution and the existing structures, when a new individual has assumed the leadership and has had some time (usually several years) to exert influence upon curriculum, courses, administrative patterns, and faculty activities, the institution will change subtly, or not so subtly, to reflect the president's views. If this is not the case, the president will probably leave the institution.[51]

Although Stout fitted this pattern well enough, he also defied it by forcing his influence onto existing structures. Instead of allowing time for his influence to permeate the system and for the system to accommodate itself as best it could to his outlook, he challenged the faculty in his first meeting with them. The faculty, just beginning to exert itself as a partner in institutional governance, immediately felt cornered. From this inauspicious beginning, both factions went on the defensive, and the chances of compromise were nonexistent. In the end, there were only two choices: remove the president or destroy the university. Consequently, Stout's departure was the best move for all concerned; he went on to various new positions, and the University of Nevada was able to recover itself and develop into a modern institution.

Epilogue

"The wolves finally 'got' Dr. Minard W. Stout, president of the University of Nevada."[1] So proclaimed the *Las Vegas Review-Journal*'s editor when he learned of the president's resignation. Perhaps, instead of the wolves, Stout's demise was the natural result of the demands of a more liberal, progressive Nevada populace and the policies advocated by such persons as Bruce Thompson, Dr. Fred Anderson, Grant Sawyer, Governor Charles Russell, and others in response to those demands. These policies, combined with the rising call for democracy, freedom, and progress on the Nevada campuses and in the nation at large, were the instrumental first steps to modernizing the state.

The principal protagonist during the traumatic 1950s at UN, Minard W. Stout, went on to a variety of positions in private industry, public education, and federal service. Stout, who claimed for the rest of his life that getting fired from UN won him the respect of many important people across the country, left Reno in early spring 1958 to become the vice president of defense planning and later vice president of research and development for the Curtiss-Wright Corporation. In 1960, he returned to the field of education as vice president for development for the University of Miami in Florida. Beginning in 1964, Stout held several posts in the U.S. Department of Education: he was director of the Student Financial Aid Branch, director of the College Program Support Branch, and chief of the State and Regional Organization of Higher Education. In 1968, he finally settled in Tempe, Arizona, where he served as professor of education and the director at the Center for the Study of Higher Education at Arizona State University (ASU). He retired from ASU and took emeritus status in 1976. All of his jobs, he argued, came to him because of his reputation for being able to "clean things up."[2]

How successful he was at "cleaning up" UN is still being debated. Whether the "small dissident group," that "central committee" of faculty troublemakers, actually won their case for participation in faculty governance or whether Nevada was at long last breaking out of its insular conservatism and joining the modern world is of limited importance. The significant fact is that the move toward becoming a viable, competitive institution in the world of higher education, which began under Stout, was by 1958 advancing so quickly that the university could never be returned to its prewar traditionalism. As an indication of that momentum, the search for Stout's replacement as the chief executive of UN relied, for the first time in the history of the university, on the formal recommendations of an elected faculty committee. The regents had devised a plan whereby the faculty committee and a committee of deans would review the applications and consider candidates for the university presidency. These two committees would submit their choices to a committee composed of three members of the faculty committee, two deans, the student body president, and the alumni director who would submit its recommendations to the board.[3]

Unfortunately, progress and politics often operate in a countervailing manner. In June 1958, three members of the Board of Regents attempted a coup d'état by trying to name the acting president, William Wood, to the permanent post of president, even though he had not been recommended by the faculty committee. For a time, the regents' attempt to reassert authoritarian control threatened to destroy the tentative and precarious governance structures developing on the campus; had their efforts succeeded, they would have reintroduced with a vengeance the dissension of the past five years. The three regents' move was not merely a case of attempting to regain authority; they were abetted by outside forces. According to one faculty member, Wood, even though he was Stout's chief lieutenant, had made some very close friends on campus, and those faculty members worked in conjunction with the regents to get him the permanent presidency.[4]

Wood, himself cognizant of the precariousness of the situation and the need for a stable administrative environment, wrote a letter that he presented to the July 11, 1958, Board of Regents meeting. In it, he requested that the board postpone the selection of a new president until after the November elections. His reasoning demonstrated a good understanding of the subtleties of the academic world. Because of the controversy surrounding the 1957 increase in the number of board members, Wood believed that any person appointed by that board would be a victim of that same controversy. In a subtle reference to the discord that had occurred when the members tried to promote him into office, he reminded the regents that someone selected by general agreement and unanimous consent would have the best chance of reuniting the campus.[5] Although the regents did not accept Wood's advice to postpone their selection, they did follow their own rules and selected someone from the list of committee recommendations. At that same July meeting, the Board of Regents elected Charles J. Armstrong to be the new president of the University of Nevada.

As is often the case when a traumatic experience has been personified, as was the turbulence of the 1950s by Minard Stout, the replacement was a very different personality than his predecessor. Armstrong was a classics scholar with a Ph.D. from Harvard who, to the delight of most of the liberal arts faculty, "was interested in academic matters." He had experience both in teaching and in administration as the president of Pacific University in Oregon. Despite the fact that he was criticized by some for working too closely with the business community and the regents and not closely enough with the faculty, most believed that he was a successful president.[6]

Furthermore, Armstrong, who served from 1958 to 1967, was able to begin the healing process as well as set the university on a path of expansion, which slowly gained momentum throughout the 1960s and 1970s. A staunch supporter of academic freedom and faculty participation in governance, he reinstated the policy of faculty committees and the all-important University Council, predecessor to the Faculty Senate. It was during Armstrong's administration, on April 25, 1959, that the AAUP removed UN from the "Censured Administrations" list. According to James Hulse, Professor Charlton Laird, one of the original five dissidents and current president of the local chapter of the AAUP, once he was satisfied that Armstrong would follow through on his policies of shared faculty governance and academic free speech, wrote to the AAUP and requested that they lift censure. Through Armstrong's and his successors' efforts, UN developed an interactive shared-governance system that would help insulate it later in the decade when campuses across the country were disintegrating.[7]

As students, too, came to share more and more in the governing process through participation on committees, access to the Board of Regents, and the passage of a "student bill of rights," their access to problem resolution helped keep future protests to a minimum. Robert Gorrell, also one of the original five dissidents, who later became the dean of the College of Arts and Science, vice president of Academic Affairs, and served as interim president in 1978, got it right when he recorded in his oral history that in response to "Stoutism," the University of Nevada became "much more democratized as a university than most institutions."[8]

Although the damage done to the university's reputation during the Stout years was slow to repair, the challenge he had presented to the liberal arts school inevitably made it more cohesive. In this respect, Frank Richardson, Robert Gorrell, Robert Hume, Charlton Laird, Thomas Little, and the others who had challenged Stout's educational philosophy were vindicated in their efforts. The University of Nevada has continued to be an exemplary model for traditional liberal arts education.[9] One result of the strengthened cohesion among faculty and the increased emphasis on liberal arts was a noticeable increase in the importance of scholarly research.

Research, other than in such applied areas as the College of Agriculture, was not well supported at UN, even before Stout's arrival. Nor was it valued by the citizenry of the state as a whole. In the mid-1940s, an article written by biology professor E. W. Lowrance on the bone structure of the musk-rat received wide national acclaim. However, it garnered only derision in the state legislature with such comments as, "What in the world did anybody care about muskrats for? The fur wasn't bad, but they weren't good to eat." It was a common belief of the more conservative elements of administration and the board, as well as legislators and much of the general public, that research interfered with a professor's real job of teaching. With the arrival of Stout in 1952, the emphasis on teaching entrenched itself even more deeply. In fact, one of the criticisms leveled against Professors Gorrell and Laird in their meeting with President Stout in April 1953 was that they wrote books. Even though it was made obvious during the Stout era that research and publishing were extraneous and even detrimental to their teaching duties, many in the liberal arts area continued to do so.[10]

Educational conservatism during the 1950s was not unique to Nevada. It was a generally held precept that the role of faculty was pedagogy. However, by the end of the decade, in institutions across the country, the academic profession began to shift its focus away from that exclusive teaching role. With the influx of new, younger faculty to campuses, Nevada's included, the pace of change accelerated during the 1960s. In addition to the new philosophies of consultative administration that were sweeping the campuses, research and publication became prominent and soon developed into major sources of social mobility for academics. Even at colleges that prided themselves on their liberal arts tradition, like Nevada, the best members of the faculty viewed academic publication and prestige as primary goals.[11] The prestige that comes to a faculty member who is recognized for his or her contribution to the discipline through research and publication reflects positively on the university.

The University of Nevada during the middle decades of the twentieth century faced the same challenges that confronted many other land-grant and state institutions: the rapid increase in student population, rapid growth born of cold war pressures, the growing pains of trying to become an institution that could serve an increasingly diverse population and rapidly expanding subject areas, and, perhaps most important, the burgeoning demand for faculty participation in the governance of the institution. In order for UN to successfully surmount these revolutions, it first had to prove to itself that it should not barricade itself behind the conservative, staid traditions that had sustained it through its first six decades. The final proof that Nevada's interests were firmly planted in the future and could not be withdrawn was the reign of Minard W. Stout. His administration attempted to straddle the past and the future by maintaining the traditional authoritarian operating ideology while promoting substantive physical development. In the end, such a combination proved unworkable. At the University of Nevada, as in the rest of the nation at midcentury, progress in one area demanded progress in all areas; the world was moving too fast for Nevada to be left behind.

But did the ordeal, public exposure, and resultant trauma actually lead to the success of academic freedom, tenure, and faculty governance on the Nevada campus? Generally speaking, the answer is a qualified yes. The academic freedoms that the faculty had known prior to the Stout administration were regained, in fact increased, but major gains accumulated more slowly. After Stout left the campus, the traumatic effects among faculty and administrators wore off quickly, even though some personal grudges remained. Many of Stout's staunchest supporters soon retired or left the campus for other positions. In general, however, department cohesion increased because the episode pointed to the need for the faculty to unify to protect their academic freedom. Similarly, such cohesion and mutual support sped up faculty governance as a basis for the operation of the university. As mentioned earlier, research and academic publishing became increasingly more acceptable, indeed, desirable. As a consequence of the newly emphasized areas of academic freedom, as well as the growing student population, more and younger faculty came to UN with the result that departments grew tremendously. One downside to the increase, even though in itself a boost to academic freedom and the viability of the university, was that a larger number of department members meant that the former system of personal agreement among a closely knit group on matters of procedure, standards, enrollment, and other important issues now had to be accomplished by a formal vote.[12]

In the long run, the university's growth, its reluctant but persistent push to gain a foothold in the progress of the postwar era, and its strong, visible affirmation of academic freedom brought it into parallel with many other liberal arts schools. Future issues of academic freedom and faculty governance, such as the University Code formalizing the procedure for termination of tenured faculty, the value of the Western Traditions program, the continued need for foreign language courses, as well as admission requirements, were fought over as determinedly as were the issues during the Stout era. The legacy of the five dissidents and their supporters, however, informed the university's progress from a local, conservative school in the 1950s to the liberal-oriented multiversity it is today.[13]

NOTES

INTRODUCTION

1. All enrollment statistics are taken from a comprehensive study of University of Nevada and University and Community College System of Nevada (UCCSN) enrollment figures from 1886 to 1999, compiled by James W. Hulse.

2. See Frederick Rudolph, *The American College and University: A History,* 487–88, for a discussion of the various approaches of colleges and universities to the issue of quality versus quantity in enrollment.

3. Ellen W. Schrecker, *No Ivory Tower: McCarthyism and the Universities,* 339; William Manchester, *The Glory and the Dream: A Narrative History of America, 1932–1972,* 498.

4. Schrecker, *No Ivory Tower,* 13–23.

5. Ibid., 17.

6. Lawrence Hanley, "Academic Freedom and National Security," 1; Robert M. O'Neil, "Academic Freedom and National Security in Times of Crisis," 22, 21.

1: DICTATORS AND "REDUCATORS"

1. Frederick M. Anderson, M.D., "Surgeon, Regent, and Dabbler in Politics," 185–86; Alice Terry, "Recollections of a Pioneer: Childhood in Northern Nevada, Work at the University of Nevada, Observations of the University Administration, 1922–1964, WICHE, and Reno Civic Affairs," 248–49; Minard W. Stout, interview by James Hulse, tape recording, January 19, 1972, University of Nevada Archives, AC 62, tape 1.

2. *Nevada State Journal,* April 30, 1952; *Nevada State News,* May 2, 1952.

3. According to both Minard Stout and Silas Ross, President Malcolm Love had encountered challenges from a small group of faculty. This group, whom Stout termed as "dangerous," had supposedly forced Love to retract his plans for expansion of the Agricultural Extension Program after he had obtained the board's approval. Therefore, the regents were looking for someone who would not be afraid to discipline these recalcitrants who were attempting to take governance into their own hands. See Silas E. Ross, "Recollections of Life at Glendale, Nevada, Work at the University of Nevada, and Western Funeral Practice," 311; Stout, interview by Hulse, University of Nevada Archives, AC 62, tape 1; and Robert M. Gorrell, "University Growing Up: Rambling Reminiscences of an English Professor and Administrator, 1945–1980," 5–6.

4. Charles H. Russell, "Reminiscences of a Nevada Congressman, Governor, and Legislator," 252.

5. For comprehensive population figures, see Russell R. Elliott, *History of Nevada,* 396. For population growth and distribution, see ibid., 325–26; and Glass, *Nevada's Turbulent '50s,* 39–40.

6. For the economic basis of the state since 1950, see Elliott, *History of Nevada,* 325–37; and Glass, *Nevada's Turbulent '50s,* 39–47.

7. Elliott, *History of Nevada,* 361.

8. Ibid.

9. For age statistics and educational levels, see Glass, *Nevada's Turbulent '50s,* 39–40.

10. Address delivered by Minard Stout on a panel about 1959 when he was with Curtiss-Wright Corporation, in James W. Hulse Papers, AC 143/65; Anderson, "Surgeon, Regent, and Dabbler," 185.

11. Hulse, *University of Nevada,* 52; *Reno Evening Gazette,* September 25, 1952.

12. Board of Regents of University of Nevada, "UCCSN Board of Regents' Meeting Minutes, January 16–17, 1953," vol. 6, http://www.nevada.edu/board/minutes/1950/1953/19530116.htm, 2–3; Everett White Harris, "My Years in Nevada: Life in Reno, a Career at the University of Nevada, Exploring the West," 70; Board of Regents Meeting Minutes, January 16–17, 1953, 2–3.

13. American Association of University Professors, "Statement on Academic Freedom and Tenure," *Bulletin of the American Association of University Professors* 34 (spring 1948): 245, cited in Robert M. MacIver, *Academic Freedom in Our Time,* 225. See also Neil Hamilton, *Zealotry and Academic Freedom: A Legal and Historical Perspective,* 375–83; and Louis Joughin, ed., *Academic Freedom and Tenure: A Handbook of the American Association of University Professors,* 98.

14. Hulse, *University of Nevada,* 52–53.

15. Hulse, enrollment statistics; *Phoenix Gazette,* May 13, 1970. This article was sent by Robert Spindler, university archivist at Arizona State University. The article describes Stout's educational philosophy. It further demonstrates that his attitudes toward the value of a classical versus a practical education had not changed from the time he was at the University of Nevada. Hulse, *University of Nevada,* 52.

16. William I. Smyth to Fredrick Wood, letter, January 17, 1953, Hulse Papers, AC 143/73.

17. Hulse, *University of Nevada,* 53; Rollan Melton, "Sonny's Story: A Journalist's Memoir," 64; Board of Regents Meeting Minutes, April 10–11, 1953, 3–5, 6.

18. The pejorative term *educationist* was used to describe someone who taught the art of teaching, rather than teaching subject matter. Such a person was the cause and result of "the domination of the American public-school system, and to an increasing extent even of the colleges and universities by the theorists of 'education for democracy,' of the school of John Dewey, who advocate an even greater quantitative expansion of institutions of higher education, without much regard for traditional disciplines or the education of the most promising young people" (*Collier's 1955 Year Book,* s.v. "academic freedom"). A more current and, therefore, less pejorative definition was given by Anthony D. Calabro in his interview with me. Calabro defined an "educationist" as one whose primary background and experience are focused on applying the methodology of pedagogy or educational administration or both as opposed to a focus on an academic discipline.

19. *Nevada State Journal,* May 28, 1953.

20. Arthur E. Bestor Jr., "Aimlessness in Education."

21. Melton, "Sonny's Story," 66; James W. Hulse, interview by author. Hulse commented that although he did not know for sure if he was actually being tape-recorded, he did make an effort to choose his words wisely. He also said that others had told him that they had had the same experience when in conference with Stout, especially if the topic was of an adversarial nature.

22. *New York Times,* May 25, 1953; *Nevada State Journal,* May 26, 1953.

23. *Nevada State Journal,* May 26, 1953.

24. Harris, "My Years in Nevada," 61, 64; Gorrell, "University Growing Up," 44–45.

25. *Reno Evening Gazette,* March 11, 1953. See also *Journal of the Assembly of the Forty-sixth Session of the Legislature of the State of Nevada, 1953,* 392.

26. *Reno Evening Gazette,* March 12, 1953; *Elko Independent,* April 9, 1953.

27. *Nevada State Journal,* March 29, 1953. The entire text of the Coulthard Committee report is printed on the editorial page. See also *Journal of the Assembly of the Forty-sixth Session,* 1953, 594–95. On Coulthard's letter to the Reno newspapers, see Thomas Little to Warren Middleton, letter, July 9, 1956, in American Association of University Professors, "University of Nevada" file.

28. See Gorrell, "University Growing Up," 45, for information about the receipt of the letters; see also *Nevada State Journal,* April 9, 1953, for information about what the letters said.

29. Gorrell, "University Growing Up," 6.

30. *Reno Evening Gazette,* April 27, 1953; *Nevada State Journal,* May 1, 1953; *Las Vegas Sun,* May 1, 1953; *Reno Evening Gazette,* April 18, 1953; Glass, *Nevada's Turbulent '50s,* 64–65.

31. Gorrell, "University Growing Up," 49, 103; emphasis in original. See also *Nevada State Journal,* April 18, 1953; and *Reno Evening Gazette,* April 18, 1953.

32. *Nevada State Journal,* April 11, 1953; Board of Regents Meeting Minutes, April 10–11, 1953, 10–11.

33. Gorrell, "University Growing Up," 58; Harris, "My Years in Nevada," 63; Melton, "Sonny's Story," 68–69; Board of Regents Meeting Minutes, June 6–7, 1953, 6.

34. Harris, "My Years in Nevada," 66–67. This same subject was discussed by Minard Stout during his taped interview with James Hulse. In it he blamed the Academic Council for curtailing President Malcolm Love's attempt to expand the Agricultural Extension Program into more areas statewide. According to Stout, Love had received the approval of the Board of Regents to proceed, only to be stymied by the refusal of the department chairs who made up the Academic Council to agree. See Stout, interview by Hulse, University of Nevada Archives, AC 62, tape 1; and Gorrell, "University Growing Up," 6–10.

35. *Nevada State Journal,* May 27, 1953; *Reno Evening Gazette,* May 27, 1953. Transcribed testimony from the Richardson hearing as printed in the "Respondent's Brief Case No. 3759" filed by the state attorney general, December 22, 1953, Attorney Gen-

eral Papers, AGO 0103/13, 14–15; *Nevada State Journal,* May 27, 1953; *Reno Evening Gazette,* May 27, 1953.

36. *Reno Evening Gazette,* May 27, 1953.

37. Harris, "My Years in Nevada," 63.

38. See, for example, Stuart J. Foster, *Red Alert! Educators Confront the Red Scare in American Public Schools, 1947–1954,* 10, for a discussion on Fisk University; and Lionel S. Lewis, *Cold War on Campus: A Study of the Politics of Organizational Control,* 55, 111–14, 231, 253, on Tulane University, Fairmont State College, M.I.T., and Barnard College.

39. Sheila Slaughter, "'Dirty Little Cases': Academic Freedom, Governance, and Professionalism," in *Academic Freedom: An Everyday Concern,* ed. Ernst Benjamin and Donald R. Wagner, 59–75; *New York Times,* May 26, 28, 1953.

40. *Nevada State Journal,* May 8, 1953; *Reno Evening Gazette,* May 1, June 5, 1953.

41. *Reno Evening Gazette,* May 5 (emphasis added), 7, 1953.

42. Lewis, *Cold War on Campus,* 25.

43. *New York Times,* May 28, 1953.

44. *Reno Evening Gazette,* February 26, 1953.

45. *Nevada State Journal,* February 26, 1953.

46. *Reno Evening Gazette,* February 26, 1953. According to a *Nevada State Journal* article on February 26, 1953, Reynolds was concerned that Communists were behind the attempt to pass legislation to legalize interracial marriages in Nevada. He is quoted as saying, "Communists have espoused such legislation to cause turmoil."

47. Anderson, "Surgeon, Regent, and Dabbler," 187; Gorrell, "University Growing Up," 47.

48. See "The Rights and Responsibilities of Universities and Their Faculties: A Statement of the Association of American Universities," 6; Albert Fried, ed., *McCarthyism: The Great American Red Scare, a Documentary History,* 140–42; Lewis, *Cold War on Campus,* 14–15; and *Reno Evening Gazette,* April 10, 1953. See Lewis, *Cold War on Campus,* 253, for a discussion of this issue at Barnard College.

49. Louis Budenz, "Do Colleges *Have* to Hire Red Professors?" 11; emphasis in original.

50. *New York Times,* May 28, 1953.

51. *Reno Evening Gazette,* May 27, 1953. For complete coverage of the hearing, see *Reno Evening Gazette,* May 25, 26, 27, 1953; *Nevada State Journal,* May 26, 27, 28, 1953; and the transcription of the minutes of the hearing located in the University of Nevada Archives. For a transcript of the hearing before the Board of Regents on the dismissal of Frank Richardson, see University of Nevada Archives, May 25, 26, 27, 1953, 205; *Nevada State Journal,* May 27, 1953; and *Reno Evening Gazette,* May 27, 1953.

52. *Nevada State Journal,* May 27, 1953; *Reno Evening Gazette,* May 27, 1953; Gorrell, "University Growing Up," 54.

53. *Reno Evening Gazette,* May 27, 1953; *Nevada State Journal,* May 27, 1953; *New York Times,* May 28, 1953.

54. Terry, "Recollections of a Pioneer," 308–9.

55. See, for example, Lewis, *Cold War on Campus,* 2–3, 35; and Jane Sanders, *Cold War on the Campus: Academic Freedom at the University of Washington, 1946–64,* 73, 108, 113.

56. *Nevada State News,* April 30, 1953. The article that McCulloch refers to is J. B. Matthews, "Communism and the Colleges." In the article is a statement that can be directly related to the comment Heward made to the *New York Times* reporter that "serving as an officer of an organization with the stupid policy it shows toward communism, a policy it has reaffirmed, militates against [Richardson's] fitness as a teacher." Matthews, after presenting the AAUP's policy on Communists being allowed to teach, says, "The statement is infused with unbelievable ignorance. False assumptions are implicit from start to finish. The recognized representatives of American college and university teachers have taken the acid test—and flunked!" (139).

57. Leslie B. Gray to George Pope Shannon, letter, May 4, 1953; Shannon to Gray, letter, May 13, 1953; Helen G. Wittenberg to Shannon, letter, May 21, 1953, all in American Association of University Professors, "University of Nevada" file.

58. Shannon to Gray, letter, May 20, 1953, in ibid.

59. Ralph E. Himstead to Minard W. Stout, telegram, May 21, 1953, in ibid.

60. See note 38 above; for comments on the types of charges initiated against faculty members, see Lewis, *Cold War on Campus,* 109–10; and Schrecker, *No Ivory Tower,* 241–64.

2: WHO IS THE BOSS, ANYWAY?

1. *Reno Evening Gazette,* June 11, 1953; Harris, "My Years in Nevada," 66; Edward A. Olsen, "My Careers as a Journalist in Oregon, Idaho, and Nevada, in Nevada Gaming Control, and at the University of Nevada," 171; John Sanford, "Printer's Ink in My Blood," 334.

2. *Reno Evening Gazette,* June 10, 1953; *Nevada State Journal,* June 5, 1953; *Reno Evening Gazette,* June 5, 1953; *New York Times,* June 6, 1953; *Nevada State News,* June 11, 1953. Edward A. Olsen confirms that the regents had already decided the fate of Richardson before they met in executive session. He states that the replaying of testimony tapes during the session was mostly for show ("My Careers as a Journalist," 175).

3. *Nevada State Journal,* June 11, 19, 1953; *Reno Evening Gazette,* July 10, 1953; *Nevada State Journal,* July 22, 1953; *Reno Evening Gazette,* July 10, 1953.

4. *Reno Evening Gazette,* July 10, 1953; *Nevada State Journal,* June 19, 1953; *Reno Evening Gazette,* October 1, 1953.

5. *Reno Evening Gazette,* December 22, 1953; "Respondent's Brief," case no. 3759, filed December 23, 1953, Attorney General Papers, AGO 013 [AGO 0085/3], 37, 39. The decision came in the case of *The National Labor Relations Board, Petitioner, v. Local Union No. 1229* and was handed down on December 7, 1953; "Respondent's Brief," case no. 3759, 38.

6. Olsen, "My Careers as a Journalist," 176; Ed Reid and Ovid Demaris, *The Green Felt Jungle,* 125.

7. *Las Vegas Review-Journal,* quoted in *Reno Evening Gazette,* June 6, 1953.

8. *Reno Evening Gazette,* June 6, 1953.

9. Sidney Hook, "The Long View," in *In Defense of Academic Freedom,* ed. Sidney Hook, 14.

10. *U of N Sagebrush,* May 8, 1953.

11. *Las Vegas Review-Journal,* quoted in *Reno Evening Gazette,* June 6, 1953; *Reno Evening Gazette,* July 14, 1954; *Las Vegas Sun,* June 3, 1953; *Elko Independent,* June 25, 1953.

12. *New York Times,* May 25, 1953; MacIver, *Academic Freedom,* 238.

13. Gorrell, "University Growing Up," 106; Exhibit A from the "Petition for *Writ of Certiorari,*" case no. 3759, filed June 18, 1953, Attorney General Papers, AGO 0103 [AGO 0085/3].

14. *Reno Evening Gazette,* July 20, 1953; *Nevada State Journal,* July 22, 1953; *Reno Evening Gazette,* July 20, 1953.

15. *Reno Evening Gazette,* June 5, 1953; *Nevada State Journal,* June 5, 1953; *New York Times,* June 6, 1953; unidentified letter titled "FACTS," in Hulse Papers, AC 143/73. See also Anderson, "Surgeon, Regent, and Dabbler," 196; Melton, "Sonny's Story," 68; Board of Regents Meeting Minutes, June 6–7, 1953, 7; *Nevada State Journal,* June 7, 1953; and *Reno Evening Gazette,* June 8, 1953. Crumley quote is from *Nevada State Journal,* June 7, 1953.

16. *New York Times,* July 12, 1953; *Nevada State News,* July 16, 1953; *Reno Evening Gazette,* August 1, 1953; *Nevada State News,* July 16, 1953.

17. *Reno Evening Gazette,* August 1, 1953; *Nevada State News,* August 6, 1953; Stout quoted in Board of Regents Meeting Minutes, December 10–11, 1953, 6, which states the grant amount was $19,480; *Nevada State Journal,* December 10, 1953.

18. Board of Regents Meeting Minutes, December 10–11, 1953, 5.

19. Ibid.; *Nevada State Journal,* December 11, 1953; *Nevada State News,* May 6, 1954; *Reno Evening Gazette,* May 4, 1954; Terry, "Recollections of a Pioneer," 256; Board of Regents Meeting Minutes, March 12–13, 1954, 1.

20. *Reno Evening Gazette,* April 24, 1954; Stout, interview by Hulse, University of Nevada Archives, AC 62, tape 1; Board of Regents Meeting Minutes, March 12–13, 1954, 2.

21. For a comprehensive discussion of the creation and expansion of schools and colleges during the Stout administration, see Hulse, *University of Nevada,* 52–70.

22. Edward S. Parsons, "Charrette! The Life of an Architect, Part I," 313–14.

23. Lewis, *Cold War on Campus,* 197; Schrecker, *No Ivory Tower,* 122; American Association of University Professors, "Academic Freedom and Tenure in the Quest for National Security," in *The American Concept of Academic Freedom in Formation: A Collection of Essays and Reports,* ed. Walter P. Metzger, 64, 105.

24. Terry, "Recollections of a Pioneer," 308–9; Ross, "Recollections of Life at Glendale," 298; Schrecker, *No Ivory Tower,* 185, 186.

25. Schrecker, *No Ivory Tower,* 185, 186.

26. Ross, "Recollections of Life at Glendale," 298–99; *Reno Evening Gazette,* April 12, 1953.

27. *Reno Evening Gazette,* October 13, 1953; *Nevada State Journal,* October 14, 1953.

28. Board of Regents Meeting Minutes, October 13–14, 1953, 6; *Nevada State Journal,* October 14, 1953.

29. *Nevada State News,* November 12, 1953.

30. *Nevada State Journal,* November 6, 1953; *Reno Evening Gazette,* November 6, 1953; Harris, "My Years in Nevada," 65.

31. Gorrell, "University Growing Up," 95. See also Board of Regents Meeting Minutes, December 10–11, 1953, 4; *Reno Evening Gazette,* November 6, 1953; *Nevada State Journal,* November 6, 1953; and *Nevada State News,* November 12, 1953. The entire statement reads: "In order to dispel any concern that might be felt by the people of the State regarding the attitude of members of the staff of the University of Nevada on Communism, I hereby affirm that I am not a member of the Communist party or affiliated with such party. I do not believe in, and I am not a member of, nor do I support any organization that advocates the overthrow of the United States Government by force or other unconstitutional methods." Gorrell, "University Growing Up," 95.

32. Harris, "My Years in Nevada," 63.

33. *Journal of the Assembly of the Forty-seventh Session of the Legislature of the State of Nevada, 1955,* 47. For the history of AB 44, see ibid., 47, 61, 71, 81, 220, 246, 254; and *Journal of the Senate of the Forty-seventh Session of the Legislature of the State of Nevada, 1955,* 54, 134, 135, 147, 172. The information on the governor's signature and the history of AB 44 after it was enrolled in the *Nevada Revised Statutes* was obtained through telephone and e-mail discussions with research clerk Nan Bowers of the Legislative Council Bureau on July 31 and August 1, 2001. After signature, the bill was enrolled into three separate sections of the *Nevada Revised Statutes:* 281.330 for public employees, 391.310 for schoolteachers, and 396.320 for university personnel. Further investigation shows that in 1967, Senate Bill 115 included a section that repealed the statute for schoolteachers. The other two, however, are sill on the books, if somewhat amended. See *Nevada Revised Statutes,* [part 1:20:1955] + [10.8:37:1887; added 1959, 199]-(NRS A 1969, 1434; 1993, 3420).

34. *Reno Evening Gazette,* November 6, 1953; *Nevada State Journal,* November 6, 1953.

35. *Reno Evening Gazette,* December 8, 11, 1953; *Nevada State Journal,* December 11, 1953; Edwin R. Bayley, *Joe McCarthy and the Press,* 104.

36. *Reno Evening Gazette,* December 11, 1953; Harris, "My Years in Nevada," 63; Gorrell, "University Growing Up," 96.

37. *U of N Sagebrush,* quoted in *Reno Evening Gazette,* December 23, 1953; Schrecker, *No Ivory Tower,* 125.

38. Board of Regents Meeting Minutes, December 10–11, 1953, 6; *Reno Evening Gazette,* November 6, 1953; *Nevada State Journal,* November 6, 1953.

39. University of Nevada, Office of the President, "Faculty Bulletin no. 410," Governor Charles H. Russell Papers, GOV 0291, "University of Nevada Correspondence, 1954."

40. *Reno Evening Gazette,* April 21, 1954; *Nevada State Journal,* April 21, 1954; *New York Times,* April 21, 1954.

41. *Elko Independent,* June 25, July 8, 1954; *Reno Evening Gazette,* April 21, 1954.

42. *Reno Evening Gazette,* May 25, 1954; "FACTS," in Hulse Papers, AC 143/73.

43. Hulse Papers, AC 143; *Nevada State Journal,* November 30, 1954.

44. Harris, "My Years in Nevada," 68–69.

45. Ibid.; Gorrell, "University Growing Up," 60–61; *U of N Sagebrush,* May 25, 1955; Tony Angell, "In Memoriam: Frank Richardson, 1913–1985," 812.

46. *Nevada State Journal,* January 10, 1954; Barbara Jean Brown to Russell, letter, January 16, 1954, Russell Papers, GOV 0291, "University of Nevada Correspondence, 1954"; "FACTS," Hulse Papers, AC 143/73.

47. Allvar H. Jacobson to Silas E. Ross, letter, February 16, 1955, Russell Papers, GOV 0295, "University of Nevada, 1955." See also "Academic Freedom and Tenure: The University of Nevada," app. 2, second draft, for information on the Jacobson letter; and on Dean Wood's meeting, see Charlton G. Laird to Warren G. Middleton, letter, July 7, 1956, both in American Association of University Professors, "University of Nevada" file.

48. On attendees at the special executive session, see "Academic Freedom and Tenure," app. 2; and Laird's letter to Middleton, both in American Association of University Professors, "University of Nevada" file.

49. *Reno Evening Gazette,* February 25, 26, 1955.

50. Anonymous letter to Russell, February 28, 1955, Russell Papers, GOV 0295, "University of Nevada, 1955"; Russell to E. Allan Davis, letters, April 9, 1956, November 12, 1957, Russell Papers, GOV 0291, "University of Nevada–Reno, 1957"; Charles H. Russell, "Message of Governor Charles H. Russell," *Appendix to Journals of Senate and Assembly of the Forty-eighth Session of the Legislature of the State of Nevada, 1957,* 1:5. See also Anderson, "Surgeon, Regent, and Dabbler," 193; and *Reno Evening Gazette,* January 23, 1957.

51. *The University of Nevada: An Appraisal—the Report of the University Survey,* vi, hereafter called *McHenry Report.*

3: LET THE INVESTIGATIONS BEGIN

1. Gorrell, "University Growing Up," 76–77; emphasis in original. This anecdote was related to Gorrell by Anatole Mazour who had taught Russian history at UN in the 1940s. See chap. 1; and Gorrell, interview by author.

2. *Nevada State Journal,* March 1, 1955; *U of N Sagebrush,* March 4, 1955.

3. *Reno Evening Gazette,* February 26, 1955, May 22, 1954. See also Glass, *Nevada's Turbulent '50s,* 70. Anonymous political ad for Bruce Thompson in Hulse Papers, AC 143/73.

4. Glass, *Nevada's Turbulent '50s,* 67; Arthur E. Orvis, radiogram, Russell Papers,

GOV 0295, "University of Nevada, 1955"; E. C. Wallenfeldt, *American Higher Education: Servant of the People or Protector of Special Interests?* 43.

5. Lewis, *Cold War on Campus,* 208, 269; Hamilton, *Zealotry and Academic Freedom,* 28.

6. *Nevada State Journal,* March 6, 1955; *Reno Evening Gazette,* March 7, 1955; *Nevada State Journal,* March 10, 1955; *Reno Evening Gazette,* March 10, 1955; *Nevada State Journal,* March 8, 1955.

7. *New York Times,* March 6, 1955; *Reno Evening Gazette,* March 7, 1955.

8. *Reno Evening Gazette,* March 7, 1955.

9. *Reno Evening Gazette,* March 15, 1955; *U of N Sagebrush,* March 18, 1955; alumni president Samuel B. Francovich to Governor Charles H. Russell, Russell Papers, GOV 0295, "University of Nevada Correspondence, 1955"; *Nevada State Journal,* March 15, 1955; *Reno Evening Gazette,* March 15, 1955.

10. *Reno Evening Gazette,* March 15, 1955.

11. *Nevada State Journal,* March 15, 1955; *Reno Evening Gazette,* March 15, 1955; *Nevada State Journal,* March 18, 1955; *Reno Evening Gazette,* March 18, 1955. For the history of SB 270, see *Journal of the Senate of the Forty-seventh Session,* 395, 412, 423, 472, 473, 494; and *Journal of the Assembly of the Forty-seventh Session,* 558, 559, 596, 601, 614, 617, 632, 657. For the governor's signature, see *Reno Evening Gazette,* March 23, 1955; and *Nevada State Journal,* March 23, 1955.

12. *Nevada State Journal,* March 27, 1955.

13. Ibid., April 3, 1955; Board of Regents Meeting Minutes, April 2–3, 1955, 9; "Letter from S. E. Ross to A. C. Grant," Minard W. Stout, biographical file.

14. *Nevada State Journal,* March 27, 1955.

15. Harris, "My Years in Nevada," 64.

16. Ibid., 65; "Report of Committee Named to Define Those Individuals Having the Privilege of Voting on Matters Coming before the Faculty Forum," General Faculty Meeting Minutes, AC 101/3/16.

17. *Nevada State Journal,* April 23, 1955.

18. *U of N Sagebrush,* April 29, 1955; *Nevada State Journal,* April 23, 1955.

19. *U of N Sagebrush,* May 6, 1955.

20. Ralph E. Himstead to Victor L. Jepsen, letter, June 23, 1953; Russell R. Elliott to Himstead, letter, July 1, 1953, both in American Association of University Professors, "University of Nevada" file.

21. Himstead to Robert B. Brode, telegram, July 16, 1953; Brode to Himstead, telegram, July 20, 1953; Himstead to Eugene H. Wilson, telegram, July 16, 1953; Wilson to Himstead, telegram, July 17, 1953; Austin E. Hutcheson to Himstead, letter, September 9, 1953; Ralph H. Lutz to Himstead, letter, August 26, 1953, all in ibid.

22. George Pope Shannon to Leslie B. Gray, letter, September 24, 1953; Frank Richardson to Himstead, letter, October 26, 1953, both in ibid.

23. Shannon, "Statement to the Council, Relative to University of Nevada Situation," February 4, 1954; Brode to Shannon, letter, March 16, 1954, both in ibid.

24. Shannon to Brode, letter, March 25, 1954; Brode to Shannon, letter, March 29, 1953; Chester F. Cole to Himstead, letter, May 31, 1953, all in ibid.

25. Himstead to Stout, telegram, March 26, 1954; Shannon to Himstead, memo, March 29, 1954, both in ibid.

26. Schrecker, *No Ivory Tower,* 314–37; *Chicago Tribune,* April 27, 1954; *Reno Evening Gazette,* May 5, 1954; Schrecker, *No Ivory Tower,* 319–20. See also *Collier's 1956 Year Book,* s.v. "academic freedom," for a discussion of the AAUP's reluctance to censure administrations because of private arrangements between institutions and complaining scholars. This was not the case at UN in the 1950s, though it is one more explanation of the reluctance of the AAUP to use its censure power in the cause of academic freedom.

27. Schrecker, *No Ivory Tower,* 322–33; Walter Metzger, "Ralph F. Fuchs and Ralph E. Himstead: A Note on the AAUP in the McCarthy Period," courtesy of Jordan E. Kurland, associate general secretary of the AAUP.

28. Charles G. Howard and Glenn A. Bakkum to Ralph F. Fuchs, letter, June 25, 1956, in American Association of University Professors, "University of Nevada" file; *Nevada State Journal,* June 3, 1955; *New York Times,* June 5, 1955; Gorrell, "University Growing Up," 77; *Nevada State Journal,* June 1, 3, 1955.

29. Stout, interview by Hulse, University of Nevada Archives, AC 62, tape 1; *Nevada State Journal,* October 20, 1955.

30. Bakkum to Warren C. Middleton, letter, May 12, 1956; Bakkum to Fuchs, letter, June 26, 1956; Howard to Middleton, letter, May 12, 1956; Howard to Middleton, note, July 5, 1956, all in American Association of University Professors, "University of Nevada" file.

31. Stout, interview by Hulse, University of Nevada Archives, AC 62, tape 1.

32. Kirk, *Academic Freedom,* 100; William F. Buckley Jr., *God and Man at Yale: The Superstitions of "Academic Freedom,"* xi.

33. Stout, interview by Hulse, University of Nevada Archives, AC 62, tape 2. All of the information in this paragraph was taken from tape 2 of this three-tape series. That Stout received and wrote a response to the AAUP report and that it contained many errors are supported by two articles in the *U of N Sagebrush,* February 10, October 12, 1956.

34. Robert A. Hume to Middleton, letter, July 8, 1956, in American Association of University Professors, "University of Nevada" file; Denver Dickerson, "Salmagundi," *Nevada State News,* April 26, 1956.

35. Dickerson, "Salmagundi," *Nevada State News,* April 26, 1956.

36. G. C. Wheeler to Middleton, note, July 9, 1956; Helen C. White to Middleton, note, July 25, 1956; George R. Stewart to Middleton, note, July 23, 1956; Charlton G. Laird to Middleton, letter, July 7, 1956; Frank Richardson to Middleton, letter, July 22, 1956; Hume to Middleton, letter, July 8, 1956; Robert M. Gorrell to Middleton, letter, July 11, 1956; Thomas M. Little to Middleton, letter, July 9, 1956; Harold N. Brown to Middleton, letter, July 9, 1956, all in American Association of University Professors, "University of Nevada" file.

37. Stout to Fuchs, letter, August 20, 1956; George Stewart to Fuchs, letter, August 21, 1956, both in ibid.

38. Gorrell, "University Growing Up," 78, 81; Stout, interview by Hulse, University of Nevada Archives, AC 62, tape 3; *U of N Sagebrush,* May 17, 1957.

39. Board of Regents Meeting Minutes, June 5–6, 1945, 1; Harris, "My Years in Nevada," 69–70; *U of N Sagebrush,* September 23, 1955. During the time that the existing rules were suspended, the procedure for obtaining tenure was "evaluation and recommendation by the Departmental Head to the Dean of the College, who will make recommendation to the President for submission to the Administrative Council, and then to the Board of Regents." See also *Reno Evening Gazette,* June 5, 1954; and *Nevada State Journal,* June 6, 1954. Both newspapers also list the requirement that the applicant must be approved by his fellow faculty before any of the other steps can be taken.

40. *Nevada State Journal,* June 3, 1955; *Reno Evening Gazette,* June 7, 1954.

41. A. Taxpayer, "For the Next MEETING of the Board of Regents," Russell Papers, GOV 0295, "University of Nevada Correspondence, 1955."

42. *Reno Evening Gazette,* June 11, 1955; *Nevada State Journal,* June 12, 1955.

43. Stout, interview by Hulse, University of Nevada Archives, AC 62, tape 1; *Nevada State Journal,* June 7, 1955.

44. Stout, interview by Hulse, University of Nevada Archives, AC 62, tape 1; *Nevada State Journal,* June 8, 1955. The twenty-one-point criteria were: professional preparation of the individual; teaching effectiveness; professional interest in and counseling of students; punctuality and dependability in discharge of duties; scholarly production; professional reputation; evidence of professional growth; cooperation as a faculty team member; leadership and initiative in the promotion of the university program; participation in extra duties (such as committees); attendance at university lectures, concerts, plays, and social and athletic events; participation in faculty activities; participation in developing good public relations; attitude on the job; integrity; judgement, tact, and common sense; ability to work with others harmoniously; professional ethics; physical health, energy, and alertness; mental health and stability; and personal appearance. Stout, interview by Hulse, University of Nevada Archives, AC 62, tape 1.

45. *Nevada State Journal,* June 7, 1955. See also Stout to Russell, letter, February 23, 1956, with attached copies of a letter from Stout to Newton Crumley and three newspaper articles, in Russell Papers, GOV 0291, "University of Nevada Correspondence, 1956."

46. *Nevada State Journal,* June 8, 1955.

47. Ibid., June 12, March 22, September 2, 4, 1955; *Reno Evening Gazette,* March 22, June 11, September 2, 1955; Glass, *Nevada's Turbulent '50s,* 69.

48. *Reno Evening Gazette,* September 3, 1955; *Nevada State Journal,* September 4, 1955; Elko editorial quoted in *Reno Evening Gazette,* September 15, 1955; Ross, "Recollections of Life at Glendale," 312.

49. *Nevada State Journal,* September 23, 1955.

50. *Reno Evening Gazette,* September 3, 1955; *Nevada State Journal,* September 4, 1955.

51. *Reno Evening Gazette,* September 3, 23, 1955; *Nevada State Journal,* September 23, 1955; *U of N Sagebrush,* October 21, 1955.

52. *Nevada State Journal,* September 23, October 1, 2, 1955; *Reno Evening Gazette,* September 23, October 1, 1955.

53. *Reno Evening Gazette,* October 3, 1955.

54. Ibid., October 8, 12, 13, 1955; *U of N Sagebrush,* October 14, 1955.

55. *Nevada State Journal,* October 20, 1955; *Reno Evening Gazette,* October 20, 1955; "Senate—October 19, 1955" minutes of the ASUN-Stout meeting, Hulse Papers, AC 143/73.

4: OUT WITH STOUT

1. *U of N Sagebrush,* April 1, 1957.

2. *Nevada State Journal,* October 20, 1955.

3. Terry, "Recollections of a Pioneer," 309; Gorrell, "University Growing Up," 102, 107.

4. *U of N Sagebrush,* November 11, 1955; *Nevada State Journal,* January 19, February 26, 1956.

5. *Nevada State Journal,* November 8, 1955, February 26, January 19, 1956; *U of N Sagebrush,* November 30, 1956; *Highlights of Progress,* American Association of University Professors, "University of Nevada" file.

6. *Reno Evening Gazette,* January 16, 18, 25, 1956; *Nevada State Journal,* January 11, 1956.

7. E. Allan Davis to Governor Charles H. Russell, letter, April 15, 1956, Russell Papers, GOV 0291, "University of Nevada Correspondence, 1956."

8. *U of N Sagebrush,* April 20, May 11, 1956.

9. Ibid., April 29, 1956.

10. *Reno Evening Gazette,* February 16, 17, 1956.

11. *U of N Sagebrush,* January 6, 1956; *Nevada State Journal,* January 8, 1956; Stout, interview by Hulse, University of Nevada Archives, AC 62, tape 1.

12. *Reno Evening Gazette,* March 6, 20, 1956; Melton, "Sonny's Story," 69; *Nevada State Journal,* March 20, 1956; *U of N Sagebrush,* March 23, 1956. Melton, a student himself during the Stout administration, claims that more than 300 students were involved. The local papers, however, set the number at between 150 and 200.

13. Bob Ferraro, interview by author.

14. "University Students Go on the Warpath," news release copy from the *White Pine News,* April 4, 1915, in Hulse Papers, AC 143/80; emphasis added; Hulse, *University of Nevada,* 41, 42.

15. *Nevada State Journal,* March 21, 22, 1956; *Reno Evening Gazette,* March 22, 1956.

16. *Reno Evening Gazette,* March 22, 1956; *U of N Sagebrush,* March 23, 1956.

17. *Nevada State Journal,* March 24, 1956; *Reno Evening Gazette,* March 24, 28, 1956.

18. *U of N Sagebrush,* April 6, 1956.

19. *Nevada State Journal,* April 27, 1956; *U of N Sagebrush,* May 11, 1956; Board of Regents Meeting Minutes, June 4–5, 1955, 13–14; April 26–27, 1956, 7–8.

20. *U of N Sagebrush,* May 4, 1956; Stout, interview by Hulse, University of Nevada Archives, AC 62, tape 1.

21. Hulse, interview by author. Hulse described Silas Ross as a sensitive individual who seemed somewhat saddened by the experience of the Stout years and preferred not to discuss them. Hulse, as a reporter for the *Nevada State Journal,* covered much of the controversy at UN, and it is his recollection that as Stout's tenure lengthened, so, too, did his autocratic attitude. See also Hulse, *University of Nevada,* 58; and Stout, interview by Hulse, University of Nevada Archives, AC 62, tape 1.

22. *Reno Evening Gazette,* October 30, 1956.

23. Ibid.

24. Ibid.

25. *New York Times,* October 28, 1956. About objectivity, see Glass, *Nevada's Turbulent '50s,* 69; and *U of N Sagebrush,* October 26, 1956.

26. *McHenry Report,* 58.

27. *New York Times,* October 28, 1956; *McHenry Report,* 65; *U of N Sagebrush,* October 26, November 9, 16, 1956.

28. *McHenry Report,* 184–86.

29. Ibid., 186–93; Effie Mona Mack, "A Study of the *McHenry Report* titled 'The University of Nevada: An Appraisal,'" Attorney General Papers, AGO 0187 [AGO 0172] A 27.17, Board of Regents, University of Nevada, 1957, 4–5, 1–4, 12. The document is stamped "Received, February 5, 1957." See also *Nevada State Journal,* February 3, 1957.

30. *U of N Sagebrush,* February 15, 1957.

31. *Reno Evening Gazette,* January 18, 1957.

32. *Reno Evening Gazette,* February 28, March 5, 1957.

33. Ibid., February 28, 1957.

34. *U of N Sagebrush,* January 18, March 1, 1957; General Faculty Meeting Minutes, February 21, 1957, AC 101/3/16, 2, 3; *Reno Evening Gazette,* March 5, 1957.

35. *Journal of the Assembly of the Forty-eighth Session,* 237, 450; *Reno Evening Gazette,* March 2, January 19, 1957; *U of N Sagebrush,* March 1, February 15, 1957.

36. Wallenfeldt, *American Higher Education,* 46. See also *McHenry Report,* 53, 57, concerning the popular election of regents and preferred number of board members.

37. *Reno Evening Gazette,* January 19, 1957.

38. *Journal of the Senate of the Forty-eighth Session,* 323; *Reno Evening Gazette,* March 22, 1957; *Nevada State Journal,* March 22, 1957; *U of N Sagebrush,* March 29, 1957.

39. *Journal of the Senate of the Forty-eighth Session,* 323; *Nevada State Journal,* April 3, 4, 1957; *Reno Evening Gazette,* April 4, 1957.

40. *U of N Sagebrush,* March 15, 1957; *McHenry Report,* 58. Other ironies may be involved here in that according to Emerson's original, "An institution is the length-

ened shadow of one man . . . and all history resolves itself very easily into the biography of a few 'stout' and earnest persons" (quotes added).

41. *New York Times,* October 1, 1957; Board of Regents Meeting Minutes, May 18–19, 1957, 5; June 1–2, 1957, 3–4; August 17–18, 1957, 7.

42. *U of N Sagebrush,* September 27, 1957; *Nevada State Journal,* November 3, 1957.

43. *Nevada State Journal,* October 5, 1957; Board of Regents Meeting Minutes, November 2–3, 1957, 9.

44. *Reno Evening Gazette,* November 4, 1957.

45. Ibid.; *Nevada State Journal,* November 3, 1957.

46. *Nevada State Journal,* November 3, 1957; *Reno Evening Gazette,* November 4, 1957; Board of Regents Meeting Minutes, November 2–3, 1957, 9; *Nevada State Journal,* December 6, 15, 1957. For the entire structure of the committees as planned by the regents for the selection of a president, see the December 6 issue.

47. Stout, interview by Hulse, University of Nevada Archives, AC 62, tape 3; Ross, "Recollections of Life at Glendale," 221.

48. General Faculty Meeting Minutes, October 24, 1957, AC 101/3/16, 1–2 of attachment; Terry, "Recollections of a Pioneer," 312.

49. *Nevada State Journal,* November 10, 1957. This issue contains a comprehensive report on Stout's interview.

50. Board of Regents Meeting Minutes, December 18–19, 1957, 1; *Nevada State Journal,* December 29, 21, 1957.

51. Paul Westmeyer, *An Analytical History of American Higher Education,* 166.

EPILOGUE

1. From the editorial written in the *Las Vegas Review-Journal* and reprinted in the *Nevada State Journal,* October 13, 1957.

2. Stout, interview by Hulse, University of Nevada Archives, AC 62, tape 1; professional résumé in Stout, biographical file; *Reno Gazette-Journal,* March 25, 1994, obituary notice for Minard W. Stout, who died on March 23, 1994; Terry, "Recollections of a Pioneer," 315.

3. Hulse, *University of Nevada,* 59; Glass, *Nevada's Turbulent '50s,* 69; *Nevada State Journal,* December 15, 1957.

4. Gorrell, "University Growing Up," 124. Gorrell relates that a faculty member promised that Wood would give him (Gorrell) the vice presidency if he would convince those regents whom he knew well to make Wood the president.

5. William R. Wood to A. C. Grant, letter, July 10, 1958, Russell Papers, GOV 0291, "University of Nevada Correspondence, 1958." See also Board of Regents Meeting Minutes, July 11–12, 1958, 1–3.

6. Gorrell, "University Growing Up," 126; Hulse, *University of Nevada,* 59–61.

7. Hulse, interview by author. Hulse believes that because Laird was one of the original victims under the Stout administration, his assurance to the AAUP that the conditions had improved was sufficient for the organization to lift the censure. The concept of shared governance was relayed to me by Anthony Calabro in an oral inter-

view, April 10, 2000. In that interview, Calabro explained that the roots of shared governance were in the changes that occurred on campuses as a result of the influx of veterans under the GI Bill. These students brought with them an unshakable belief that democracy needed to exist on campus as well as in the world at large. This concept was already entrenched within the faculty. Consequently, by the 1960s, both students and faculty were insisting on an active role in the governing structure of the university. Out of that developed a true faculty role with input into the operation. What in Stout's day was a very narrow decision-making structure made up of the Board of Regents and the president came, by the late 1960s, to be a coalition of regents, administration, faculty, students, and staff, all of whose opinions were actively sought. For a discussion of campus unrest in the 1960s at UN, see Hulse, *University of Nevada,* 72–74, 127.

8. Hulse, *University of Nevada,* 213; Gorrell, "University Growing Up," 436–37.

9. Richard L. Siegel, interview by author. Siegel, a political science professor, believes that it was because of their strong liberal arts backgrounds, as well as their personal integrity and principles, that Gorrell, Laird, and others were able to maintain their independence and not "cave in" to Stout and the board's authority.

10. Gorrell, "University Growing Up," 431, 102. Gorrell and Laird had published their extremely popular *Modern English Handbook* in 1952. This text went through many editions and brought much acclaim to the university. Laird also published *The Miracle of Language* in 1953, despite Stout's stricture. Robert Hume, another of the original five dissidents, had published *Runaway Star: An Appreciation of Henry Adams* in 1951. For a fairly comprehensive list of faculty writings and publications, see Hulse, *University of Nevada,* 244–50.

11. Stanley Rothman, "Tradition and Change: The University under Stress," in *The Imperiled Academy,* ed. Howard Dickman, 27–70; Wallenfeldt, *American Higher Education,* 58. Wallenfeldt believes that publication may also make faculty more attuned to colleagues outside the institution instead of their own university. This did not seem to be the case at UN.

12. Gorrell, interview by author.

13. Siegel, interview by author.

BIBLIOGRAPHY

This study is based primarily upon a large body of university documents, including the files of the Board of Regents and the external review committee created by the state legislature. The University of Nevada Oral History Project provided important perspectives of several major figures involved in the controversy. The wealth of documentation from the American Association of University Professors provided useful insights from outside the state. Despite its importance, the issue has received scant academic attention, with two notable exceptions. Both studies, however, examine the controversy within much larger historical contexts and necessarily provide only a broad commentary. Interestingly, these two treatments aptly reflect the two major camps that existed during that academic war.

James W. Hulse first wrote about the controversy as a young reporter for the *Nevada State Journal,* and he revisited the issue in 1974 when he undertook the writing of a history of the university upon its centennial. Hulse's sentiments clearly rest with the imperiled faculty, reflective of his distinguished career as a member of the history department and his lifelong support of academic freedom. Although the historian Mary Ellen Glass does not overtly come to the defense of the Stout administration and the resolute Board of Regents in her wide-ranging study of the contentious Nevada political and economic environments of the 1950s, she takes special care to emphasize the conservative, anti-intellectual climate of opinion that was prevalent in the state at that time. Public opinion, she implies, undoubtedly greatly influenced the outlook and actions of the elected Board of Regents. Glass makes clear that during this turbulent time, genuine concerns about the philosophy and practice of education were rightfully examined, but because Nevada politics was based on close personal interaction, and truculence on both sides, the enmities and bitterness of those discussions would not dissipate.

Numerous archival collections informed this study. Especially useful were the papers of the Friends of the University that provided the extreme anti-Stout viewpoint, the Minard W. Stout audiotapes for the opposite view, the minutes of the Board of Regents that provided the administrative view, and the James W. Hulse Papers that provided a comprehensive collection of all points of view. The papers of the state attorney general were valuable for their focus on the legal aspects of the controversy as well as the state supreme court appeal proceedings. The Governor Charles H. Russell Papers provided a variety of aspects on the controversy and some of the politics behind it. The files from the AAUP were extremely helpful in providing the view of the academic institution from outside the state.

Oral histories, though extremely insightful, must be used with caution; hindsight is sometimes tainted with faulty memory. However, I found the oral histories of Professors Robert M. Gorrell and Everett W. Harris, presidential secretary Alice Terry, and Dr. Frederick M. Anderson to be quite beneficial. The oral history of Silas E. Ross, even though written fourteen years after he left the Board of Regents, seemed to be very judicious, though limited in its information about the dissension of the 1950s. The interviews were of great benefit because through them I was able to obtain insight into the recovery of the university and how the turbulence of the Stout era informed the future growth and attitudes of the university system.

The most extensive and consistent sources available for this study were the Nevada newspapers, in particular the *Nevada State Journal* and the *Reno Evening Gazette.* These two Reno newspapers not only had the most coverage, but their points of view were also sufficiently different to provide a contrast of opinion. Although neither was staunchly for or against any faction in the controversy, it was apparent that the *Reno Evening Gazette* was more willing to accept the administration and Board of Regents's viewpoint, at least during the first four years of the conflict. It was instructive to follow the slowly changing editorial attitude, especially after the retirement of board chairman Ross and the influx of new perspectives on the board. The evidence of change, most noticeable in the *Gazette,* was less obvious in the *Journal* because that newspaper had consistently maintained a more objective view of all sides. Other newspapers around the state provided more biased opinions; some, like the *Elko Independent,* were extremely biased. But their inclusion here shows the extent to which local personalities permeated and influenced the events at the university. The articles from the *New York Times* were also interesting in that they provided a more distant perspective on the controversy, but I am unsure if the newspaper's strong antiadministration bias was a product of its local correspondents' views or of a wider national sentiment.

The bibliography that follows identifies the sources that have been used directly in this study. Although there are many excellent studies on the subjects of academic freedom, university governance, educational administration, free speech, and McCarthyism, I attempted to employ a representative cross-section that would meld the contemporary and modern viewpoints, the conservative and liberal views, and the academic and business perspectives. Out of this mix, I hope to illuminate some of the intricacies of the internal workings of higher education in the 1950s and open up some new areas for future study.

ARCHIVAL MATERIALS

American Association of University Professors. "University of Nevada" file. George Washington University, Washington, D.C.

Attorney General. Papers. Nevada State Archives, Carson City.

Friends of the University. Papers. University of Nevada Archives, Reno.

General Faculty Meeting Minutes. 1917–1969. University of Nevada Archives, Reno.

Hulse, James W. Papers. University of Nevada Archives, Reno.

Russell, Governor Charles H. Papers. Nevada State Archives, Carson City.

Stout, Minard W. Audiotapes. University of Nevada Archives, Reno.

———. Biographical file. University of Nevada, Reno.
———. Faculty information. Arizona State University, Tempe.

GOVERNMENT DOCUMENTS

Appendix to Journals of the Senate and Assembly of the Forty-eighth Session of the Legislature of the State of Nevada, 1957. Carson City: State Printing Office, 1957.
Journal of the Assembly of the Forty-sixth Session of the Legislature of the State of Nevada, 1953. Carson City: State Printing Office, 1953.
Journal of the Assembly of the Forty-seventh Session of the Legislature of the State of Nevada, 1955. Carson City: State Printing Office, 1955.
Journal of the Senate of the Forty-seventh Session of the Legislature of the State of Nevada, 1955. Carson City: State Printing Office, 1955.
Journal of the Assembly of the Forty-eighth Session of the Legislature of the State of Nevada, 1957. Carson City: State Printing Office, 1957.
Journal of the Senate of the Forty-eighth Session of the Legislature of the State of Nevada, 1957. Carson City: State Printing Office, 1957.

PRIMARY STUDIES

Hulse, James. Compilation of enrollment figures, 1886–1999, encompassing the entire University and Community College System of Nevada.
The University of Nevada: An Appraisal—the Report of the University Survey. Bulletin no. 28. Nevada Legislative Counsel Bureau, December 1956. Carson City: State Printing Office, 1957.

ORAL HISTORIES

Anderson, Frederick M., M.D. "Surgeon, Regent, and Dabbler in Politics." Interview by R. T. King, 1985. Oral History Program. University of Nevada, Reno.
Gorrell, Robert M. "Growing Up: Rambling Reminiscences of an English Professor and Administrator, 1945–1980." Interview by Kathryn M. Totton, 1983. Oral History Program. University of Nevada, Reno.
Harris, Everett White. "My Years in Nevada: Life in Reno, a Career at the University of Nevada, Exploring the West." Interview by Mary Ellen Glass, 1969. Oral History Program. University of Nevada, Reno.
Melton, Rollan. "Sonny's Story: A Journalist's Memoir." Interviews by R. T. King and Jeanne Harrah, 1999. Oral History Program. University of Nevada, Reno.
Olsen, Edward A. "My Careers as a Journalist in Oregon, Idaho, and Nevada, in Nevada Gaming Control, and at the University of Nevada." Interview by Mary Ellen Glass, 1972. Oral History Program. University of Nevada, Reno.
Parsons, Edward S. "Charrette! The Life of an Architect, Part I." Interview by Mary Ellen Glass, 1983. Oral History Program. University of Nevada, Reno.
Ross, Silas E. "Recollections of Life at Glendale, Nevada, Work at the University of Nevada, and Western Funeral Practice." Interview by Mary Ellen Glass, 1970. Oral History Program. University of Nevada, Reno.

Russell, Charles H. "Reminiscences of a Nevada Congressman, Governor, and Legislator." Interview by Mary Ellen Glass, 1967. Oral History Program. University of Nevada, Reno.

Sanford, John. "Printer's Ink in My Blood." Interview by Mary Ellen Glass, 1972. Oral History Program. University of Nevada, Reno.

Terry, Alice. "Recollection of a Pioneer: Childhood in Northern Nevada, Work at the University of Nevada, Observations of the University Administration, 1922–1964, WICHE, and Reno Civic Affairs." Interview by Mary Ellen Glass, 1976. Oral History Program. University of Nevada, Reno.

INTERVIEWS BY THE AUTHOR

Calabro, Anthony D. Reno, April 10, 2000.

Ferraro, Bob. Reno and Boulder City, June 21, 2000.

Gorrell, Robert M. Reno, July 8, 2003.

Hulse, James W. Reno, April 7, 2000.

King, R. T. Reno, March 16, 2000.

Siegel, Richard L. Reno, April 4, 2000.

NEWSPAPERS

Elko Independent, 1953–1954.

Las Vegas Review-Journal, 1953.

Las Vegas Sun, 1953.

Nevada State Journal, 1952–1957.

Nevada State News, 1952–1956.

New York Times, 1953–1956.

Phoenix Gazette, 1970.

Reno Evening Gazette, 1952–1957.

Reno Gazette-Journal, 1994.

U of N Sagebrush, 1953–1957.

SECONDARY SOURCES

Association of American Universities. "The Rights and Responsibilities of Universities and Their Faculties: A Statement of the Association of American Universities." Princeton: Association of American Universities, 1953.

Angell, Tony. "In Memoriam: Frank Richardson, 1913–1985." *Auk* 103, no. 4 (October 21, 1986): 812.

Bayley, Edwin R. *Joe McCarthy and the Press.* New York: Pantheon Books, 1981.

Benjamin, Ernst, and Donald R. Wagner, eds. *Academic Freedom: An Everyday Concern.* New Directions for Higher Education, no. 88, winter 1994. San Francisco: Jossey-Bass, 1994.

Bestor, Arthur E., Jr. "Aimlessness in Education." *Scientific Monthly* 75, no. 2 (August 1952): 109–16.

Buckley, William F., Jr. *God and Man at Yale: The Superstitions of "Academic Freedom."* Chicago: Henry Regnery, 1951.

Budenz, Louis. "Do Colleges *Have* to Hire Red Professors?" *American Legion Magazine* (November 1951): 11–13.

Commager, Henry Steele. *Freedom Loyalty Dissent.* New York: Oxford University Press, 1954.

Dickman, Howard, ed. *The Imperiled Academy.* New Brunswick, N.J.: Transaction Publishers, 1993.

Elliott, Russell R. *History of Nevada.* Lincoln: University of Nebraska Press, 1973.

Foster, Stuart J. *Red Alert! Educators Confront the Red Scare in American Public Schools, 1947–1954.* Counter Points: Studies in the Postmodern Theory of Education, vol. 87. New York: Peter Lang, 2000.

Fried, Albert, ed. *McCarthyism: The Great American Red Scare, a Documentary History.* New York: Oxford University Press, 1997.

Glass, Mary Ellen. *Nevada's Turbulent '50s: Decade of Political and Economic Change.* Nevada Studies in History and Political Science, no. 15. Reno: University of Nevada Press, 1981.

Hamilton, Neil. *Zealotry and Academic Freedom: A Legal and Historical Perspective.* New Brunswick, N.J.: Transaction Publishers, 1995.

Hanley, Lawrence. "Academic Freedom and National Security." *Academe* 89, no. 3 (May–June 2003): 2.

Hofstadter, Richard. *Anti-intellectualism in American Life.* New York: Vintage Books, 1962.

Hook, Sidney, ed. *In Defense of Academic Freedom.* New York: Pegasus, 1971.

Hulse, James W. *The University of Nevada: A Centennial History.* Reno: University of Nevada Press, 1974.

Joughin, Louis, ed. *Academic Freedom and Tenure: A Handbook of the American Association of University Professors.* Madison: University of Wisconsin Press, 1967.

Kirk, Russell. *Academic Freedom: An Essay in Definition.* Chicago: Henry Regnery, 1955.

Lewis, Lionel S. *Cold War on Campus: A Study of the Politics of Organizational Control.* New Brunswick, N.J.: Transaction Books, 1988.

MacIver, Robert M. *Academic Freedom in Our Time.* New York: Gordian Press, 1967.

Manchester, William. *The Glory and the Dream: A Narrative History of America, 1932–1972.* New York: Bantam Books, 1975.

Matthews, J. B. "Communism and the Colleges." *American Mercury* 76, no. 352 (May 1953): 111–44.

Metzger, Walter P. "Ralph F. Fuchs and Ralph E. Himstead: A Note on the AAUP in the McCarthy Period." *Academe* (November–December 1986): 29–35.

———, ed. *The American Concept of Academic Freedom in Formation: A Collection of Essays and Reports.* The Academic Profession: The Arno Press Collection. New York: Arno Press, 1977.

O'Neil, Robert M. "Academic Freedom and National Security in Times of Crisis." *Academe* 89, no. 3 (May–June 2003): 21–24.

Reid, Ed, and Ovid Demaris. *The Green Felt Jungle.* New York: Pocket Books, 1964.

Rudolph, Frederick. *The American College and University: A History.* New York: Alfred A. Knopf, 1962.

Sanders, Jane. *Cold War on the Campus: Academic Freedom at the University of Washington, 1946–64.* Seattle: University of Washington Press.

Schrecker, Ellen W. *No Ivory Tower: McCarthyism and the Universities.* New York: Oxford University Press, 1986.

Wallenfeldt, E. C. *American Higher Education: Servant of the People or Protector of Special Interests?* Contributions to the Study of Education, no. 9. Westport, Conn.: Greenwood Press, 1983.

Westmeyer, Paul. *An Analytical History of American Higher Education.* 2d ed. Springfield, Ill.: Charles C. Thomas Publisher, 1997.

INDEX